'Rahil's story of transformation is a w...
grace of God working in a person's li...
Nicky Gumbel, Vicar of Holy Trinity Bro...

'I laughed and cried as I read Rahil's phenomenal journey through life. As one living in India from a similar background, the questions Rahil asked were similar to those that haunted me for so many years.

'This brilliant book is a must-read for everybody, whatever belief system you come from, whether you are an Easterner or a Westerner. I encourage you to pick it up with reverence and see for yourself if it answers your questions about truth and joy. I cannot commend this book highly enough.'
Shanti, Iris Ministries India

'I remember the first time that I met Rahil. I was overwhelmed by the depth of this man, attracted to the peace which he carried but also aware of a beauty about him which I knew was his life's journey. This book is like meeting him again. There is depth and peace, but most importantly there is the beauty of the journey. Rahil encourages us all and draws us in to his story in such a beautiful way. As he explains, his name Rahil means "one who takes the beauty from the past into the future and leaves the bitterness behind". This is what this book will do for all who read it if they open their hearts as Rahil has done.

'Read it, enjoy it, but most importantly allow his story to become yours and for your future to become more beautiful than your past.

'Thank you, Rahil, I knew that I had met a man of peace and beauty, and now I know why.'
Paul Manwaring, Head of Global Legacy, Bethel Church, Redding, California

'Rahil's story is breath-taking. As I read it I kept wondering what would come next! It is an easy read, full of insight and shrewd observation. Above all it is an amazingly honest account of his journey to faith in Jesus, a journey with many questions and much painful stripping away, but ultimately extraordinary joy.'
Ram Gidoomal, Chairman, South Asian Concern

FOUND BY LOVE

A Hindu priest encounters Jesus Christ

RAHIL PATEL

instant
apostle

First published in Great Britain by Instant Apostle, 2016.

Instant Apostle

The Barn
1 Watford House Lane
Watford
Herts
WD17 1BJ

those cases where permission might not have been sought and, if notified, will formally seek permission at the earliest opportunity.

The views and opinions expressed in this work are those of the author and do not necessarily reflect the views and opinions of the publisher.

British Library Cataloguing-in-Publication Data

A catalogue record for this book is available from the British Library

This book and all other Instant Apostle books are available from Instant Apostle:

Website: www.instantapostle.com

E-mail: info@instantapostle.com

ISBN 978-1-909728-42-4

Printed in Great Britain

Contents

Acknowledgements

I thank the Lord Jesus Christ who sat quietly by my side as I wrote this story of my life.

I would also like to thank a myriad friends who have stood by me on this journey. Some of you were there during the 'stripping away', and others during the deep inner transition. You never judged or measured my heart, but with a kind and generous spirit you pointed me towards Jesus. You knew that He was enough.

Some friends have cried with me in tough times, and many have laughed with me as well. Each moment with you has been rewarding and refreshing. You allowed me to be me and didn't intervene. You gave grace and space for the Lord to change me, and that change beautifully continues. Wherever you are on this broad and varied canvas of my life, I am deeply grateful. You all are a wealth immeasurable.

My particular thanks to Robin Thomson for his invaluable help in shaping this book. Your wisdom and insight have been priceless on this journey.

Note: Many names in the book have been changed to protect identities.

'I am truth, I am the way, I am life'
(Gospel of John 14:6)[1]

---

[1] Author's own translation

Prologue

Our Jaguar limousine cruised into the parking bay at London's Heathrow Airport. The dark December clouds hovered over us and the wind kept biting relentlessly at the car. I completed the phone call with my PA and took a deep sigh. Of all the many flights I had taken, this trip to Mumbai was the most unsettling. Worry fogged my mind as I sat in the luxury of my car. The past year had really uprooted me. Pratap was my driver for the day, as my other cars were busy elsewhere. He and I had shared a special friendship for nearly 25 years. He knew my struggles and challenges and stood by me at all times. Very much in my inner circle, he knew a few secrets.

Pratap took out his wallet and gave me his black American Express card. 'If you need anything, don't hold back.'

As he placed the card in my hand I looked at him with a smile. 'Pratap, I'm only away for ten days. I'll be fine.'

He shrugged his shoulders and said, 'You never know, *swami*.'

I saw the trust in his eyes and remembered the countless times he had passed on his credit cards for whenever I travelled. He never asked questions as I was a close friend, and a *swami* – a revered Hindu priest – managing the European operation for one of the wealthiest and most influential Hindu organisations in the world.

'Phone me if need be,' he said.

'I will.' Feeling a little nervous, I unfastened my seat belt.

The British Airways attendants were waiting for me on the pavement. They opened my car door as they saw that I was all set. 'Mr Patel, it's good to see you again!' They were ready with their smiles and very smoothly remembered that I liked to be called by my passport name and not my priestly *swami* name.

The airline had been my choice of travel for years, and even the board members knew about my requests whenever I took their flight. They ensured that senior management took care of all my needs.

'Bye, Pratap!'

Pratap bowed his head at my feet with his knees to the ground, without any shame about who was watching, and then stood to give me a hug. I was first his *swami*, revered and worshipped. After that, his friend and companion, and he knew never to cross that boundary.

The attendants took my luggage and passport and we walked towards the terminal where a third member of the airline was waiting to check me in. I never stood in line.

'Mr Patel, we have kept your preferred seat in first class and all of the crew know that you are on the aircraft. They will ensure that you are looked after well and not disturbed in any way.' As ever, they were brilliant.

'Thank you so much,' I said.

As I stood there in my orange robes, surrounded by BA attendants, the people around me wondered who or what I was. I heard a lady ask, 'Is that the Dalai Lama?'

I smiled and muttered under my breath, 'No, dear, he's Buddhist. I'm a Hindu.'

The escort was ready and I cruised through security and entered the first class lounge.

'Sir, please take a seat. We have reserved this area for you. We will come to collect you when the flight is ready to board.'

I sat on the comfy sofa and couldn't ignore my increasing anxiety. Just then, another BA attendant walked across the room to pour me a cup of coffee. 'Would you like to read anything, sir?'

'Yes. Would you bring me the *Financial Times* and the *Harvard Business Review?*'

As the attendant walked away to bring my reading, I took a sip of my coffee and wondered what was lying ahead in Mumbai. Something didn't feel right. Something was brewing in the higher echelons of the organisation, and I couldn't put my finger on it.

I was one of the most influential priests in the organisation, and thousands across the globe knew me to be a major game-changer. I was always on guard and able to manoeuvre myself through all the politics, however tricky. Although I was young, those in high places of power never dared to get in my way. They knew I was close to Guruji. In fact, very close.

I closed my eyes to pray and meditate on Guruji. He had been my father and mother for nearly 25 years. Guruji knew everything about my life: my talents, gifts, works and all of my sins. Every mistake I had made in my spiritual walk went to him without fail. I had never hidden anything. Well, almost anything. There was one matter that I would never reveal to him.

Like me, he was a *swami*, a Hindu priest, but his role was different. He was God. His very name meant that he could bring everyone from darkness to light. Guruji was the only person who could take humanity to heaven.

I prayed, 'Dear Guruji, you are God, the supreme above all and I need you to bring me…'

'Sir, your paper and magazine.'

I roused myself from my prayer, and as the man laid the magazine by my coffee, other BA attendants arrived to take me to the plane. 'We are ready for you, Mr Patel. You'll be boarding before everybody else, as usual.'

As I stepped on to the plane, I felt that I had crossed a line in my life that I had never done before. It was eerie and uncomfortable. My heart raced further.

The captain of the aircraft welcomed me. 'Mr Patel, we are so glad you are flying with us!'

I acknowledged him. 'I'm always grateful to travel with you.' I forced a smile despite my anxiety, and the cabin crew guided me to my seat by the window.

'Sir, we have specially dedicated this gentleman from our crew to look after you throughout the journey. You will be his priority.'

I thanked the attendant and settled down.

I thought again of Guruji as I stared out of the window. Whatever the issue, I was sure he would back me. He always did. He was on my side in any dispute, and always managed to carry me out of tight corners.

'Mr Patel, would you like me to bring you something to drink?'

'Yes, please. Apple juice would be nice.' I smiled as the attendant walked away. I had enjoyed this pampering from them for most of my life, and almost once a week. They made it so easy for me to reach out to our followers across the world.

Guruji had a million followers across the globe who believed with a deep conviction that he was the supreme God above all. I had converted hundreds of people in my life to come to this belief, and I preached to thousands to increase those numbers further. My mandate was clear: build temples, build the numbers and build the funds.

As I stared at the other planes coming in to land, I remembered all the times Guruji personally took care of my simplest needs – as a child and after I had become a priest. It was a privilege to be loved by God, and now I would see him again after one and a half years, the longest separation from his company.

I looked at my hands, folded in a posture of prayer; they were twitching with anxiety. I drank a little of my juice and took some heavy painkillers with an antidepressant. I hid the medicine back in my prayer kit as I had done for years.

'Can I take the glass, sir?'

'Sure. Thank you.'

I leaned my head against the headrest and closed my eyes as the plane began to roar down the runway. I looked out of the window again to see if I could see the temple in which I had lived for nearly 15 years. I searched and searched but couldn't find it. Just then a thought occurred. 'Did I lock my office?' I had hidden a very important book amidst my array of scriptures that no one must see. If I were caught with that in my possession...

Suddenly the clouds hid everything I knew below, and that gave me an unsettling feeling of isolation. I closed my eyes again to pray.

Tomorrow I'll be meeting him. The most influential Hindu leader in the world and the God of my life.

Strangely, this personal meeting, unlike hundreds of others, had an unnerving cloud over it. I knew Guruji was waiting for me even though he was very ill. Meetings with him were very restricted, no matter who or what the issue.

I was a very rare exception. All the trustees and senior priests knew that I needed no permission to enter Guruji's chambers. I was always given privacy within those four walls where nobody else took the chance to enter. Guruji would always put aside everything to meet with me. A thousand other priests in the organisation never had that privilege, and I was sure many secretly coveted my easy access.

Although the flat bed was the most comfortable device at that altitude, as always I had the most restless sleep. The voices and arguments in my sleep were back again, loud and noisy. Dark figures were hiding behind doors, watching me. I felt an electric current run through my body and I gave a scream.

'Mr Patel?'

I awoke with a slight shock. 'Yes?'

The fear must have been apparent on my face, but the crew member continued to smile. 'We will be landing shortly at Mumbai airport. Can I arrange your seating and put away your blankets?'

I forced a smile. 'Sure… thank you.'

We landed smoothly and the sun was scorching the Indian soil as it did for most of the year. The year would end in a few days' time, bringing 2012 into my life with another monotonous routine.

'Sir, the ground staff are waiting for you at the door.'

I calculated that within the next three hours I would be sitting face to face with my closest friend, father and god. The man who had changed my life.

'Thank you. You guys have been wonderful.'

After showing my gratitude, I made my way to the door of the aircraft to step on to Indian soil. I was planning to be there for just ten days, and then back to London and the comforts of my office. I didn't know that my plan was about to change drastically.

I cleared Customs easily, with the help of the BA staff, and just then I remembered that I must present my gifts to Guruji when I met him: an exclusive foot cream by Guerlain, an expensive perfume by Yves Saint Laurent to spray on his clothes, and a box of Belgian chocolates for his personal attendants. I was known never to arrive empty-handed. I had played a pivotal role in bringing style and class to Guruji's image.

My car was parked at the arrivals bay, and I finally left the efficient management of BA for the chaos of Indian traffic. As the car horned and dodged its way to the temple, I closed my eyes to pray a little more. My thoughts were already in the chambers of Guruji's room, and I was rehearsing my lines and ensuring that I missed nothing as I spoke to him. I didn't know what to expect and the driver was very silent, which added to the mystery of the meeting.

After an hour or so, we parked in the temple ground and I was led by the temple porter to my room that stood a staircase below Guruji's chambers.

I took a shower and went down to bow to the images in the temple and pay my respects. I knew I couldn't eat until I had seen the face of Guruji. It was disrespectful to eat without first seeing his face and lying prostrate before him. He had already been informed by his personal secretary that I had arrived, and had begun to prepare for our meeting.

He was writing letters, I was told, and the whole of the senior management of priests were in town.

I knew I would be asked some very tricky questions. A few of the senior *swamis* had eyes and ears all over the world and had their ways of finding out any piece of information they required. I was going to deny everything. I had spent years in the system and knew how to navigate. I wasn't easily cornered.

My key strategy was to get to Guruji first, have a meeting with him in private, and in that cover all the angles. Then I could handle anyone.

As I climbed the final flight of stairs towards Guruji's room, the head of welfare was standing at the top. 'Welcome, dear friend. How was your flight?' I could see concern on his face, and as I bowed down at his feet I decided I would say as little as possible. He was a good man and had always warned me throughout my life to tread carefully.

My problem was that I had a very inquisitive and sharp mind. 'My flight was nice, thank you.'

He took me to his office. 'This time you will not be meeting Guruji alone.'

His expression changed as if he knew I would challenge that. I knew something was brewing in the corridors of power, so I resigned myself to the idea, and said, 'Fine, so be it.'

He continued, 'We have a few questions to ask you.' Before I could even think of what they might know, he began to reveal the content of a phone conversation with a trusted friend of mine in the USA. My pulse rate shot up. Just then, from across the corridor, Guruji's personal secretary opened the door of the chamber and came out.

'Well, hello there.' He spoke in his usual deep and slow voice.

I replied with courtesy. 'Hello, *Swamiji*.'

This priest had been Guruji's personal secretary for more than 30 years. He was the J Edgar Hoover of the organisation and knew everyone's secrets. He had mastered the art of keeping his mouth shut, whatever the case. This was the reason why Guruji held on to him for so long.

'He is waiting for you.' After a pause, he said, 'My advice to you is very simple. Whatever is discussed and asked of you… just submit and agree.'

This was it. I now knew that this was as serious as I had felt it would be. At that moment, the CEO of the organisation walked along the corridor and gave me a brief welcome. He was Guruji's chief advisor in all matters, and had been adorned in orange robes for nearly 50 years. As I bowed and placed my forehead to his feet, he began to speak in his soft and yet authoritative voice.

'Hello, *swami*. I heard from London that your flight was smooth. So glad that you arrived on time.'

I stood up and looked at him with my hands folded in respect. 'It was a very good flight, thank you.'

He nodded. 'As is always the case with you,' he said with a smile, and then the smile suddenly vanished. 'We will need to discuss your recent stay in America. Shall we go in?'

The meeting had been meticulously orchestrated. A lot of homework had gone into arranging all the key questions that were going to come my way.

I knew that a lot was hanging on the next few hours. I stared at the door in front of me and knew that my time had come.

As the door slowly opened, I could smell the fragrance of fresh flowers from the inner chamber of Guruji's room. With my heart racing rapidly, I began my walk.

Chapter 1
Early days and settling down

'Mitesh! You have to go with Dad to the cash and carry! Hurry and get ready!' It was my typical Saturday call and the most challenging chore. My elder brother, Raj, shouted out my name as he left to help my mother stack the shelves with food and cigarettes in our newsagent's shop in Deanshanger near Milton Keynes. Bored and grumpy with this routine, I put on my shoes and made my way obediently to the car.

Yes. Mitesh was my childhood birth name. How it evolved into Rahil is an interesting story with many twists and turns.

I sat in the front seat of our blue Datsun Bluebird at the tender age of four with my model aeroplane that Raj had beautifully made. Like my dad, Gujarati Indians in general had a passion for Datsuns. These cars, made in Japan, had ample space and were very reliable; they would last for years. In an era in England when there were no laws on how many persons you could have in a car, as well as not having to fasten your seat belt, it was the ideal car for an Indian family to fit many people into – almost the extended family!

Me, I loved planes. That was my passion. I stared at them in the sky every day as I played in our front garden, wondering how they made straight clouds behind them that stayed there for such a long time. It was a fascinating way to daydream. Concorde had just made its first commercial trip to Bahrain in that year of 1976, and so I eagerly searched for it in the sky, hoping to see it fly over me.

With me still pondering and dreaming, we left the driveway for our local cash and carry, where Dad stacked the car with crisp boxes and crates of Coke. As he continued filling the car with cigarettes and biscuits to sell in our newsagent's shop, I stood there watching with amazement how he managed not to leave the slightest space. Every inch was utilised. Yes, that's how we Gujaratis did and still do many things. Maximise on everything; no waste, lots of gain.

In those early years, while I was fixated on my new Corgi toy cars and playing with my Hornby train set, my dad, I noticed, worked very hard along with my mum, who was a continuous and incredible support to him. At that age I didn't know that my parents were rebuilding a life from shattered dreams in Kenya here in the land of England. We had a small bungalow linked to our shop on a little hill that I thought was quite pretty. Deanshanger was a small village, and from our house we could basically see all the houses beneath us, as well as Raj's school down the road. This made me feel rather special and quite the conqueror above all. But I don't think that my parents thought of it that way. They had seen much bigger and better homes.

Gujarat is a state in North West India which borders with Pakistan, three other states and the Arabian Sea. It's roughly the same size as Great Britain and today is both agricultural and very industrial. It now contributes nearly a quarter of India's GDP and historically housed the very first office of the East India Company in the coastal city of Surat in 1608.

My great-grandfather moved from Gujarat to Kenya in 1898. He left with a group of British civil servants who were building the railways across East Africa. Kenya, Uganda and Tanganyika (now Tanzania) were British colonies back then, and so the three together were popularly known as East Africa. A lot of Gujaratis migrated to these beautiful lands in that era for a better financial future, and continued to do so for decades. So, although I'm Gujarati Indian, my ancestors spent most, if not all, of their lives in Kenya.

My grandfather (my father's father, 'Dada') was an interesting man who loved people and showed it in many ways. Very loyal and trustworthy, he was courageous and loved to take risks. He was born in 1920 in India after my great-grandfather had returned, once his work in Kenya had finished. At the age of 18 my grandfather followed his passion for business and travelled from India to Kenya in a *dhow*, which in those days was almost the only option. The journey took 40 days along the coastal areas and was very challenging. Nine out of ten of the passengers died during the journey, from Blackwater fever. The captain looked at my grandfather and said, 'Get ready. You'll be next. Any final wishes?'

My grandfather replied, 'Yes. May I have a glass of champagne?' He had his glass and he very much survived!

He saw his survival as significant and felt he was destined for a purpose, as the boat came into harbour on the beautiful sandy coast of Mombasa, known as the gateway to Kenya. After settling down amongst friends, he started his first job in the capital city, Nairobi, working as a messenger for British Army officers. It was a simple and very menial job but he gave good attention to detail and timing.

By this time, Kenya had thousands of Gujarati Indians living there, and they were well established in various industries. The British government encouraged the movement of Indians around its empire to help build industry and infrastructure in the lands they had conquered. My grandfather saw the many opportunities for growth, and so after marrying my grandmother he acquired a job as a driver for a Patel construction company that was doing fairly well in the early 1940s. Weekly he would gather with other Patels to share a bottle of beer and chat about their futures. He had big dreams and hopes and was known as a man of his word. After a lot of hard work, he received a breakthrough in 1946 when he established his own construction company. After that, his name very quickly rose to fame within government circles. His first project was a petrol station, which was a huge success, and after that he built many more across Kenya in a very short time. This led on to primary schools, military barracks, hospitals, social clubs and, interestingly, the VIP lounge at Nairobi International Airport. At the height of his empire he had 4,000 people working for him, and the family's wealth was obvious.

My father is the eldest of four and my mother is the eldest of three. They were both born in Kenya and spent most of their lives in that land where they had an arranged marriage, decided only six days before by their respective parents. Again, no wasting of time in anything! Arranged marriages were normal in that era. Indian parents would thoroughly research the other family into which they might be marrying their child. They would ask many questions regarding finance and behaviour on behalf of their child, and if need be pay a visit to the school and ask the teachers how the boy or girl they were intending would marry their child actually behaved. All the family members would get a chance to ask the boy or girl questions, all together, in one room! You may call it an interview or an interrogation. I call it both, but it was normal then, as it was a very important decision. And families wanted the best for their children. Over the generations this has changed, with Indian parents, especially in the West, giving more freedom for their children to choose their own future partners. There is more flexibility and acceptance from

Indian parents to see their child marry into different cultures, too.

After marriage, my parents enjoyed a lavish standard of living, owing to my grandfather's hard work and success. He had bought a 200-acre piece of farmland which he converted into a family resort. It was brimming with cashew nut trees, plums, pears, mangoes and pomegranates. It was the ideal place to host family meetings and big, lavish parties. My grandad was not an alcoholic, but he enjoyed his drink. His three Alsatian dogs were named accordingly, with great thought, Whisky, Gin and Sherry! They went wherever he went. That's how he liked it, and in the home he kept his favourite Congo African Grey parrot. It spoke fluent Gujarati, of course! Even our parrot had to have an Indian side to it.

My grandfather bought his first Rolls-Royce with three other Mercedes-Benz cars to add to his extensive foreign car collection by the early 1950s. These were in the driveways of several stately homes which he owned, with lush acres of land around them. Soon the whole extended family were travelling in style between India, the UK and Kenya.

All my father's siblings had some form of higher education, even though they were involved in the flourishing business. My dad acquired a pilot's degree from Oxford Air Training School, which later helped the business when they were doing large developments for the US government in the jungles of Africa. Dreams were big and hopes were high. The future was bright with abundant wealth ready to pass on and multiply from generation to generation.

Raj and I were to receive all of this, and much more. Until one day everything crashed in an instant.

During the early 1960s, political affairs in Kenya were restless, and the cry for independence was very evident. There were many complex and understandable issues between the

British, Indians and local East Africans, one of which was the Indians' wealth. The growth of money and business was catching an unhealthy eye. So, alongside talks with the British, African groups within the government were targeting wealthy Indian families.

One afternoon my grandfather received a phone call from the government to inform him that his company would be one of many to be stripped down immediately. On hearing this sudden and shocking news, my grandfather, whom I never got to see or know, passed away from a fatal heart attack at the age of 52. My father was in a state of shock after his death and didn't have much time to put affairs in place. Suddenly and very swiftly the crumbling of our business empire had begun. With not a penny left over after all the winding down, my father was left with a big family and no support, comfort, or the security that he had been so used to.

This happened within months, and all my mum and dad had left were two British passports. So the UK was the destination to build a new future.

Other family matters still had to be settled, so my parents were travelling back and forth between Nairobi and London for a few more years. This led to my elder brother, Raj, being born in London and I, four years later, in Nairobi.

Starting life again in a new land wasn't easy. My childhood was full of my mum and dad working 16 to 18 long hard hours a day in our newsagent, selling newspapers, cigarettes and foods. It was a stark difference for them, from lavish homes and cars to stacking shelves. As I hadn't seen their wealth, I found it difficult to understand why they had to work so hard with endless hours.

After filling our lovely Datsun to the brim, we made our way back to our shop where I stood and watched as my dad, mum and brother unloaded the boxes and crates into our garage. We never used the garage for our car. It was a storage space that was not to be wasted! It was common sense.

Many Gujarati Patels acquired and ran newsagents in the 1970s and 1980s. It was an easy route into business which allowed an excellent cash flow alongside the very hard work. Newsagents very quickly became synonymous with our surname.

'Are you all related?' my friends would ask.

'No!'

Gosh, I thought. Can there be no other common name besides Smith or Jones?

The name 'Patel' reaches back nearly 600 years where it was initially 'Path-Likh', 'Path' meaning tablet of stone and 'likh' meaning 'to write'. Historically and traditionally our role and skill was to write the accounts for the various kings and princes across the then 300 kingdoms of Gujarat. This skill continued over generations and developed into various businesses. Patels became successful wherever they went in the world. Their entrepreneurial history in East Africa gave the banks in the UK an ease and confidence in the 1970s and 1980s to back our businesses very quickly. The Gujarati culture, where all family members contributed to the business, whatever it might be, gave them then – and still does today – the advantage of saving money and ensuring that trust levels never had to be measured.

My mother was not very good at English in her very early years in Deanshanger, but was very astute in maths. Not a penny in the till went unaccounted for and so her contribution was huge, not to forget the way she looked after our home and food requirements.

So for a few years my dad and mum ran the shop well and he paid off all the loans from the bank rather quickly. Raj was at school and I was at home, playing with planes.

We always had guests and relatives in our home, which is typical of Gujarati Patel culture. Food is always available and there was never a need to be invited. The doorbell would ring and the next batch of people would enter our home, and the smell of *masala chai* and home-made biscuits would be in the air. Shop work, noise and spicy Indian food for guests were the general themes of the household whilst growing up. Every now and then we followed the news where a certain Margaret Thatcher was hoping to be Prime Minister. Her strong personality and piercing words shot out of our television frequently. My dad would have a discussion after the news with his brothers and I'd just sit there, uninterested in politics. I was a kid, after all.

During these many visits from friends and family, I remember a friend by the name of Deepak who came to meet my father. He was telling him about a certain spiritual 'guru' from India coming to town. Would our family like to host him for an afternoon?

In those days my dad, Raj and I ate meat and my dad enjoyed a glass of red wine now and then, too. Many Hindus don't eat meat or drink alcohol as a part of their faith. We weren't devout Hindus. We never went to a temple except once in a blue moon for some festival – and that was only to socialise and receive the latest gossip from the world of Patels.

My dad said yes and a few days later a blue car turned up at our home with a group of men wearing orange robes.

'Why are they wearing that?' I asked my dad.

'Don't ask many questions, son, and don't say that we eat meat. OK?'

He was really hoping that I wouldn't open my big mouth and let slip that I loved my eggs and sausages! I was only four, and this was a bit weird. I stood by our porch overlooking our front garden, and the scene with these orange men was like a sci-fi film

29

where the aliens land on earth for an invasion. I got very scared and ran into my room. Peeping round the door, I saw them all singing and chanting, applying red powder to each other's foreheads. I refused to come out, with the threat that I would start crying. Finally they left and I was still alive.

After some time in Deanshanger my dad acquired a clothes business in Belgium and the whole family stayed there for a year. Raj went to an American school as I played at home on my own.

At the end of the year my father decided it would be better to go back to London for the sake of our education. Education and academia were very important in the Indian community. They would not only define your future but the class level of family into which you could marry. Parents like mine would sacrifice, work harder and do whatever they could to ensure that their children had a high standard of education.

My dad knew that Deepak was living in a lovely leafy suburb in north-west London. It had a very high 'class' of English community and he was drawn to that. Dad always wanted Raj and me to learn as much as we could from the local British. He felt they had incredible gifts of management, administration and diplomacy. That was the only way a tiny island could have held a massive empire spanning one quarter of the earth's land mass for around 300 years. He was fascinated by that, as I would be years later. Not only that, but Deepak's two children, Jaymin and Sanjay, went to a very good state school that wouldn't cost money. It was ideal – in his eyes.

Initially, Deepak said that we could live in their home until we found our footing. The eight of us would cram into a semi-detached house within walking distance of the school.

So that was our destination. It became my home town from the age of five until 19. It was here that all the twists and turns in my life began.

Chapter 2
Influences of two worlds

Elvis Presley had just died at the age of 42 when we re-entered British life in 1977. I didn't know much about him at my age except that he was all over the news and thousands were crying. My dad mentioned his death to Raj one afternoon as we were settling our belongings in our new home.

Day-to-day life in our joint home was a tricky affair. For me, it resembled a finishing school, and sometimes Alcatraz!

Deepak and his family believed in discipline, order and hierarchy. I lost out in all three. The strict house rules were boring, the table manners frustrating, and to add to that I was the youngest of them all and so the hierarchy was suffocating. I had the short straw in everything.

For most Indian families, it has been a tradition that the eldest is prepared and trained to manage the family affairs once the parents retire. So the youngest is almost seen as a substitute if things go wrong. It's like being option two if option one fails. I was option two.

My guess is that if I had sat with the family all those years ago and asked, 'What does love mean to you?' the discussion would have been very stagnant. Both my parents and Deepak and his wife would have shown their love by the way they provided the best of things – in other words, education and a nice home.

Anything more than that in the area of love would be a discussion that wouldn't even start. Of course, this was normal for their generation, and not only in our Asian culture.

So the time at Deepak's home was a training ground for me to come to terms with anything and everything that the wise and experienced elders put me through. After all, it was for the greater good!

Looking back now, I realise that they really did mean it for my good. And perhaps they felt that I needed their training. But it's never easy to be the youngest, and at the time I found it all too hard.

'You're making too much noise with your teeth when you eat with that spoon!'

Sanjay, the younger of the two brothers, was the apple of his parents' eyes, intelligent and very confident. I noticed that he was outperforming his elder brother in most areas, and that's how he became option one and the favourite.

'Pull the food from the spoon with your tongue and lips. No noise!'

That evening at the dinner table everyone's focus suddenly turned to me. My family, his family. Dead silence. It felt like I was on stage and ready for a performance. As they all stared, I had to show the refined way to eat from a spoon. I was only five! I still made a scratchy noise very slightly with my teeth.

'Try again.'

Sanjay sat there patiently until I got it right. Eventually, I was allowed to leave the table, a bit disturbed by the whole commotion over teeth on a spoon.

From now on, Sanjay, his elder brother and his parents were my mentors. Throughout my early childhood they would have a huge say in my life as Dad and Mum were busy settling into our new newsagent's business in the local area. Home was like a prison with 24-hour guards. Deepak and his family believed that discipline and order would surely lead to success. Love, affection, intimacy or even noticing and recognising the treasure in me were never on the list. I had no idea if that way of life was true or false.

I had to wash my hands before sitting on the sofas. No feet were allowed on them. If an elder walked into the room I was ready to sit on the floor. Addressing elders and guests with finesse and a gentleman's manners was a must – all that was missing was the curtsey! It was endless and I was too young and I hated it. The whole household felt it was their duty to train me. I was being refined externally, but my deeper needs of love were not being met.

Sanjay was a great public speaker as well as very academic. This dynamic within the household was constantly pushed upon me and I had to follow suit, except that my stage performance was nearly every hour of the day, at home. I always had to be on form and brilliant at everything. None of my movements would go unnoticed. Every aspect of my life was checked and examined. Exam results would be seen and discussed by both families. Years later, I came home with ten As and one C. You can guess what was acknowledged and recognised. The C!

Little did I realise then that this watch over all my moves would be a constant throughout my years ahead, in a wild and crazy way.

The new VHS and Betamax recorders had been launched shortly before our move to London, so our families enjoyed an array of Indian Bollywood movies every Friday night. For me that was a task! Not understanding Hindi as well as the others did, and a typically prolonged Bollywood movie meant that I sat in front of the television screen for three and a half hours with the most confused face. Why such a long film? I thought. Can't they be short and simple?

We all had to sit together and 'enjoy' this most boring affair. In those years, Indian families did everything together. Slipping away to have some fun in private was not permitted. For parents, traditions and particular ways of doing family life had to be grasped by the next generation. Anything different or which involved a change from the general mould was met with fear and concern. Part of this was the fact that Asian families coming to Britain, not entirely by their own choice, wanted to hang on to their traditions and keep their young people from becoming too much like the 'English'. They wanted things to be just like 'back home', not realising how that had already changed so much.

I could also see in those very early years how difficult it was for my parents to be living with another family, highly dependent, without much freedom. It was a stark difference from the life of luxury they had lived in Kenya. My mother had learned how to drive in a Mercedes-Benz especially bought for her. She had never known what lack was, and now she had to catch the bus to make any journey. No chauffeurs, no cook, no night watchman, no cleaners and servants roaming a stately home 24 hours a day.

I would sit at times and ponder over photographs from Kenya. The comfort and luxury were astounding. Raj at my age was wearing three-piece suits. I saw the remnants of that lifestyle when I went back during summer holidays to visit my cousins. My dad's sister had married into a very wealthy family, and I could see quite clearly that they didn't have to lift Coke crates or crisp boxes. It was laughable to see my cousin ask the house servant to pump the punctured tyre of his bike!

'Can't you do that yourself?' I remember asking. He gave me a weird look. It wasn't normal for them to do such things.

As I didn't know that life in Kenya, my challenges were different to my parents'. I had other things to get accustomed to. I struggled with the insistence on visiting the Hindu temple each weekend in north London. I would cry again and again with a deep passion to stay at home and not attend. I was never asked, just told that I must go. What for? That explanation was never given. I had never seen such people in orange clothes before, and it all seemed so alien to me. Every Saturday I had to pull off the same drama and so there were times when Sanjay's father, Deepak, would stay behind at home with me. The tears did their magic most of the time, but somehow there were weekends where I had no choice.

The temple was an old converted church building with a red and white façade painted by the community to bring some colour. There was a Hindu flag representing that particular denomination perched on the top. Most of the time, though, it stayed slumped and never swayed.

The word 'Hindu' has its roots in a geographical location derived from the Indus valley where the river Sindh was flowing many centuries ago. The Persians pronounced this 'Hindh' and referred to the people living beyond the river as 'Hindus', from which came the names 'India' and 'Indians'. It was a geographical, not a religious term. In this vast region, which today is split between Pakistan and India, the British in the eighteenth and nineteenth centuries found the remnants of this ancient civilisation worshipping many gods in many ways. They coined the term 'Hinduism' to describe the beliefs, customs and practices of the peoples of India. All starting from the river and word 'Sindh'.

Hinduism as a faith is actually a canvas with hundreds of religions, most of them as diverse and different from each other as Christianity would be from Buddhism. Some Hindu denominations eat meat and others don't. Most Hindu denominations believe that the body has a soul but quite a few don't. Some groups in India still have animal sacrifices in their temples, whereas others would never have heard of such a thing and would obviously believe it to be quite wrong. Many Hindu organisations build beautiful temples for their gods, but some make a very small shrine in a village and worship their deity in the simplest way. Philosophically and doctrinally, there are vast differences in their views of the nature of God and man's existence on earth.

The temple denomination which my family joined along with Deepak was very strict on not eating meat or drinking alcohol. Meat was believed to carry forward the emotions of the animal into one's own life, and alcohol would lead to a lack of discernment and judgement. This 'instability' would disallow one to focus on God and family. It was a very basic rule that all had to obey fervently in order to lead a godly 'Hindu' life.

Temples help to build communities. When Indians migrated to the West all those years ago, the first issue they tried to solve was to find a community of people with a similar cultural background. Seeking a particular denomination wasn't on the agenda. The temple helped people gain a sense of belonging in a new country full of English people whose culture and way of life were too different to explore or imbibe. In this way, people looking for a place to *belong* eventually found a place of *belief*.

My parents initially went out of an obligation to Deepak's family, as we were staying in their home. It wasn't their choice. They also wanted to be accepted and liked. As time went by, our family increasingly experienced the sense of 'belonging', but I continued to resist.

I remember one Saturday I stood by the temple at the bottom of the steps, refusing strongly to go inside. My family were in there somewhere. I could hear the singing and chanting, and the ringing of bells. It was crowded and stuffy. I was happier outside and simply stood on my own – quite stubborn for a kid. Just then, a boy came over and asked me, 'Why don't you come inside?'

'Don't want to.'

'Just come!'

'No.'

He was much taller than me, and with a smile took a firm grip of my hand and began to drag me up the steps with an expression that suggested he was doing me a favour! I shouted at him to get off me. I tried pulling away, but no matter how hard I tried, I just kept going higher up the steps. At the very top I fell to the ground in the struggle. I shouted and swore at him. I remember that very well, as his face was full of shock. He left me alone and ran inside. Swearing was seen as an evil act. Defiant and victorious, I went back down the steps until the very end of the meeting.

I was successful for many months, but over time my resistance became futile. My family were beginning to enjoy the community and were making more and more friends with similar stories and backgrounds from Kenya. I remember my dad waking me up at five o'clock every morning when the 'guru' in orange came to London. Everyone called him Guruji, and he was the voice and face of God. The word 'guru' in the ancient Sanskrit language means one who takes you from darkness to light. That's what we all called him, and believed it, too.

Almost all the Hindu denominations have a guru who would be the conduit of some sort to God for the community. Each would most firmly believe that theirs was the one and only pathway to God. When our Guruji came to London from India, our whole community would rally around him and be at the temple every morning and after work in the evening.

I had a struggle waking up, going to the temple, bowing to Guruji and then going to school. It was like boot camp minus the push-ups.

But I remember one morning when my father was talking to Guruji. In the middle of the conversation, Guruji turned to me as I held my dad's hand. 'Do you like eating mangoes?'

'Yes,' I said.

He told his attendant to fetch me a mango. I was surprised that he even noticed me. He cared, and although he was talking to my dad, he diverted his attention and found me equally important. What did he see in me then? I was only seven! The attendant brought the mango and Guruji cut it himself and fed me. I was very impressed with that instant moment of compassion.

But apart from mangoes, waking up and the whole process of going to the temple to watch Guruji perform various rituals was a bore. Dad was in awe and fully focused on this man in orange who was God on earth, while I quietly slept on his lap. How strange that I was not keen or interested like the other kids my age. They were so tuned in and I hadn't the foggiest idea about the faith or anything about these orange people, except that one of them was very important. I still ate meat at school. I wasn't to tell anyone, though. Mum made sure that was a secret. We could not eat meat if we wanted to be members of this particular temple community. It was severely frowned upon and a gateway to hell for many, so I had to learn by heart certain lines: 'No, I don't eat meat. Not even eggs!' What was the big deal? I thought. Eggs and bacon are a must in the morning.

These very normal and laid-back views of mine would change radically as my parents became more and more plugged into the temple and its community. Dad became very firm in his faith, which led to him having a meeting with the head teacher at my primary school. Very soon I was on packed lunches filled with boring sandwiches or a vegetarian *biriyani* from the night before! I watched my friends enjoy their hot meaty dinners. Sad and feeling lonely, I ate what I had and pretended to them that I was fine with it. A packed lunch led me to sit on my own in a different area. Soon lunchtimes became an embarrassing affair which I didn't look forward to.

A dinner lady approached me one day and asked, 'Are you alright, my child?' Just then a tear rolled down my cheek. I was with all my friends and yet not really with them... An ongoing theme that years later would continue to haunt me.

Eventually, my desire for meat disappeared completely and I learned how to cope with lunchtimes. I just pretended that I was fine. Pretence would be something I'd develop very well as time passed by.

Apart from this single aspect, my school years were heaven. The infant and primary school had a beautiful location on top of a hill, surrounded by stunning countryside views. The school was linked with the local comprehensive, with its vast rugby fields only a few minutes down the road. School years were full of great moments with friends and teachers. I loved my teachers. They were very helpful and arranged wonderful events to keep us engaged.

My brother Raj, Sanjay and I were the only non-white students. Raj was four years senior to me so I hardly saw him. Even so, I had no hassle from anyone throughout my school years. I was glad for that. Only once a slightly bigger boy was hassling me after school hours for a few days, and so I told Raj. That was it. He followed this boy after school one evening while I stood and watched from a distance. My brother, calm as ever, with his school bag in one hand, lifted the boy up by his collar with his other and threw him into the hedge! It was swift and smooth. Raj was particular about his dark blue school uniform, which was unharmed in the event. I beamed. After that, it was clear that I was never to be messed with.

This strange, protective yet distant love from Raj would continue for the rest of my years with him. Raj taught me many things outside of school hours as the years drifted by, and was keen to have me ahead of the others in class. He struggled when he was teaching me how to tell the time, but strangely found it easy to teach me how to solve the Rubik's Cube which had just won the toy of the year award (in 1980). We played with those Rubik's Cubes day and night as well as stringing horse chestnuts and baking them for conker fights.

School continued to excite me, and my very special moments were at Christmas-time when I got to take part in the nativity play. I was always chosen to be one of the wise men. It was such a joyous time with carol singing, tree decorating and good food. Making angels from gold and silver paper, using cardboard to build a typical house in Israel – it all excited me. Singing hymns every morning was a regular matter throughout the school year. I'd sing loudly. At home, whilst playing with my toys, I'd sing one prayer over and over again: 'Our Father, who art in heaven, hallowed be your name…' It was my favourite.

One of my favourite toys at home was a British Airways model plane. I remember very well swinging that in the air and singing this prayer out loud: 'Our Father, who art in heaven…' Once, I was at the top of the stairs when I had a brief moment of a soft touch deep in my heart. I was only eight, but I remember: it felt special. So I kept singing it over and over again.

I loved prayers at school. Before lunch the prayer would be, 'For what we are about to receive, may the Lord make us truly thankful. Amen.' Before leaving to go home, another prayer session would take place after we had all placed our chairs on the tables so that the cleaners could do their task easily.

We would visit our school's local church now and then to explore, learn and draw various aspects of the church building. I remember sitting in the pews smiling at the walls as the sun shone through the stained-glass windows. I recall my drawing of a very old tombstone dating back to 1752.

In many ways, school felt more like home. I was very comfortable there. Through the years I always ranked at the top in the study of Christianity. Later, one teacher suggested that I take it up for further studies. Mr Phillips was a fine RE teacher who noticed the interest and love I had for the faith.

For the next two years, I moved between two completely different faiths on a daily basis. Christianity at school; Hinduism at home. It's strange how school felt like home and home like a school.

But by the age of ten all the passion and desire for whatever was Christian would take a huge turn and become almost extinct.

During these years of staying with Sanjay's family, my parents were very keen that everything I would do or become should be modelled around him. He was everything I was meant to be. At school, excellent. In the temple, a great speaker. It became rather weird at times.

I remember at school when the register was being read at the beginning of class. Reading the surname Patel, the teacher asked me, 'Are you related to Sanjay?'

'Not really,' I said, a bit too quickly. 'We stay together, that's all.'

The teacher beamed and said, 'Well, that's good. Because even if you're half of what Sanjay is, you'll do well in life!'

What? Are you kidding me? I couldn't believe it. I wanted to be myself! That night as the whole family were religiously watching the famous TV series *Dallas* and pondering over who shot JR, I sat and pondered on my life being shaped around another individual and how that was affecting me.

Things were changing a lot in our nation and the world at large. Margaret Thatcher finally became the first woman Prime Minister in the UK and later, on the other side of the Atlantic, the Americans chose a certain Hollywood actor by the name of Ronald Reagan to be President.

I played with my new Pac-Man video game as I pondered over the changes in my life, and wondered how much change lay ahead. The biggest influence right now was Deepak and his family, bringing change in my education, home manners, eating habits and the temple itself with all that came with it.

Little did I know that this family would one day open the door wider and with intention towards Guruji and his massive international organisation. My cycle between two faiths would be severed and I'd take that door in the most rapid and radical way.

Chapter 3
A change of heart

In 1981, we had the privilege of witnessing the wedding of Princess Diana to HRH Prince Charles.

We were as excited as all the other 750 million people watching this fairy-tale marriage of the century. Mum was more intrigued than all of us and didn't want any disturbance as she parked herself in front of our television. I stood there that morning wondering if she would ever take as much interest in me as she did in Diana. I knew that she always had a deeper interest in Raj. Maybe he reminded her of the wealthy times in Kenya, and I reminded her of a poor beginning. Dad and Raj were chatting as the wedding rolled on, and I felt excluded and inferior.

We were now in our own new home in the same area, close to the school. This home was like a sanctuary for me. The family now had more independence from Deepak's family, though we still remained close. We eagerly welcomed this, and I finally found some space to breathe. This gave room for me to spend more and more time with my dad, Raj, and now and then with Mum. Just us.

My father was a very hard-working man who ensured there was never a lack in our home, a talented and gifted man who gave my brother and me exposure to many beautiful things. By now he had moved on from his newsagent's business and very quickly became an established senior sales rep for a pharmaceutical company. He would take me on long, adventurous car journeys across the UK and suggest that I stand and watch how he would communicate and sell to clients. I remember watching him talk with incredible articulacy and confidence. He was keen for me and Raj to acquire the widest exposure to various aspects of life. My guess is that he didn't want us to be caught short as he was after his father died.

Homework from him was to watch and take notes from *John Craven's Newsround*. This was a television newsreel at 5.05pm every weekday, specially geared for children. My brother and I would collate our notes and then present the news to Dad – as thoroughly as could be, precise and articulate. My dad enjoyed listening to us both giving an array of news, and it made him proud. He didn't want us just to have good grades but to develop an astuteness politically, culturally and socially that would broaden our perception of life.

Alongside this, Dad was very calculated in what and who he allowed in my life. His way of giving us social exposure was through sports. So he would engage us on Friday evenings with indoor cricket. I became a very good batsman for a team in the Indian Asian league, playing against sides across London. Some Saturdays he and I would play squash together, where I remember him being so much fitter than me. 'Son, play smart, not hard!' he would say. What did that mean? I was dripping with sweat and gasping for breath. My dad's anxious face suggested that I was too young to be exhausted. Health concerns, which would loom so large later on, had already begun to surface.

On Sundays we would play golf as a family. In my first year at the comprehensive, Dad and Raj were passionate for me to join the school rugby team, which I did, and stayed with it for two years.

Dad's heart was for me to have an interest in a variety of areas. He was keen to meet my teachers to ensure that my school subjects were firing on all cylinders. He came to school once and had a debate with my maths teacher who felt that I wasn't capable of pursuing the subject further. 'My son will do well, and I trust him.' No pressure for me, I thought sarcastically. As usual, my opinion wasn't even on the agenda, and so I slogged away and eventually got my A grade.

Looking back, it was very sweet that my dad stood up for me against my teachers and put a lot of faith in me. This very occupied life of mine and his pursuit of business still allowed us to chill together, and so with Raj we would go to the cinema now and then and religiously eat at Pizza Hut once a week in Harrow on the Hill.

My mother was the traditional Indian housewife while we grew up. A brilliant cook, Mum would produce Mexican, Chinese, Lebanese, Italian and various Indian and Kenyan dishes. Our household functioned with unfailing rhythm owing to her management. She was a very organised lady who kept our home neat, tidy and spotless. Any fingerprints on the cabinets and there would be trouble.

I remember being in a hurry once and so I closed the door of the refrigerator with my hand not on the handle, and as a result I left fingerprints on the door. As I was going out of the front door she called, 'Going somewhere?'

'Yes.'

'Come here!'

'Why?'

'Can you see something on the door of the refrigerator?'

'Not really.'

'Take another look. Can you see those fingerprints?'

I got the message. Within seconds I was cleaning my marks.

This rhythm of education, sports and extra activities with my dad, mother and Raj continued for a few years, along with economic growth and holidays in some of the most beautiful places on earth. I'll never forget the five-day cruise we had among the Greek islands of Patmos, Rhodes and Mykonos. We had the best time ever as a family coming on and off our cruise liner, *Oceanus*. We paid regular visits to Kenya, where we enjoyed the luxuries of life with my aunt in Mombasa, and on the Maasai Mara game reserve.

But by the end of 1985, I noticed that matters in my heart had changed quite a bit.

Mum was a very religious lady who was devoted to the Hindu temple faith that we belonged to. She regularly sat by our small Hindu shrine in our home praying and asking the gods for various things. Hindus, as I'm sure many faiths, have lists of things they want in life from God, and the mothers tend to have the final edited version!

We had a whole room dedicated to our house shrine. These small, decorative wooden cabinets are a key aspect of a Hindu household, regardless of denomination. (Not all Hindus have images in their home shrines and temples, but the great majority do.) It's very important to God that he has a space and place in your home, and not just a dinky little spot under the stairs like Harry Potter! House shrines keep the family aware that every aspect of life revolves around God, who is present in the images within the shrine, and that he is listening to all our conversations and plays a part in them.

House shrines played a pivotal role in keeping the Hindu faith alive during King Ashoka's era in India centuries ago. The king promoted a lot of Buddhist practices, and Buddhism spread very fast across the whole land, but the house shrines kept the faith and identity of Hindus alive at home, which subsequently prevented mass conversion. Eventually, after King Ashoka died,

Hinduism rebirthed itself with a stronger force, vigour and growth. In the interim, the fire was kept alive by house shrines.

My brother and I built our house shrine keenly with various kinds of wood, with the help of friends, and filled it with the deities of our particular Hindu denomination. We added lots of pictures of Guruji. We went to India to select the marble images of the gods and had them sent to London. Marble is the stone that has always been used to make these images. With its white and bright glare along with its smooth and grained texture, it depicts beauty, majesty and grandeur, which is why it was used to build the Taj Mahal as well. To spend vast amounts of money by using marble is a way of expressing one's love to God, or in the case of Emperor Shah Jahan, his passion for his beautiful wife, Mumtaz.

We had a very special ceremony in our home to install our images. It's only a marble statue until you infuse the spirit of that particular god through rituals and chants from ancient scripture, when it then becomes an image in which that particular god is present. We invited senior members to do the ceremony. We gathered a lot of people on that day, sang worship songs, prayed and fed everyone well.

I was very fond of the shrine. I bathed the deities regularly, put them to sleep and decorated them with various jewels and garments. These images were now alive and needed the attention, love and care that one places on one's own body. This level of devotion allows the spirit within the image to enter one's own self to purify it.

The deities whom we worshipped represented various forces of nature, for example, the sun or the storm, qualities such as wisdom or wealth, or members of the family of gods, about whom there were many stories. They were all related in some way to the great god Vishnu, who was a manifestation of the ultimate, supreme deity, Brahman, beyond all expression or imagination. But Guruji embodied all of the family of gods. He was supreme above all, the voice and face of the ultimate God, the supreme manifestation on earth. So worshipping Guruji was a direct conduit to worshipping the almighty.

We were supposed to have only the deities that our denomination followed. But my mum found it difficult to give up the other gods that her family had worshipped for decades, and she kept them secretly in our house shrine. When friends or other *swamis* saw these images of other gods in our home, they frowned.

I spent a lot of time in that room. It was a special place for me. Yes, a huge change had manifested towards the Hindu rites and rituals after my early collisions with the faith.

This change of heart was largely a result of Guruji giving me a lot of personal attention, care and recognition during his visits to London. Finally, I was important and acknowledged, and that by God!

During these visits, I spent a lot of time at the temple with friends attending his sermons and morning prayer times. The various *swamis* who accompanied Guruji would visit our home for dinner quite regularly, and a deep friendship was formed with them and our family. I loved the way they cared for me.

Swami literally means 'master' or 'lord', and it is a title for a Hindu religious teacher or priest. In our denomination they were more like monks who had taken certain vows to serve Guruji and the community. They had a lot of respect from the community members.

This special time with them and Guruji helped my heart to incline towards everything connected with our temple and denomination.

My friend Ramesh from the temple came home one day to watch the FIFA World Cup. Mexico were the hosts in 1986, and Maradona was our star footballer. My circle of friends had changed. At 14 years old, I was now spending more time with the boys from the temple than those from school.

Ramesh turned to me during half-time and said, 'Your mum is a little worried, Mits.'

Mits was the way my friends from the temple addressed me.

'What do you mean?' I said.

'Well, you hardly mix with your schoolfriends now. You don't get involved with extra school activities as you used to. You've changed a lot.'

'I know.'

Ramesh continued, 'I remember when my older brother tried to drag you up the steps and you swore at him!'

We both laughed at the change. I replied to his concern, 'Guruji's the most important person in my life right now.'

He was stunned. 'Spend some more time with your parents, don't you think?'

I deflected his comment as the match started again.

Although Mum was a little worried with my drastic change, she continued further and further on her personal journey with God, as I did mine. She sang at our house shrine daily in the morning, and during the evenings my brother and I would attend, light the lamp and sing the *arti* prayers to our gods. This was a regular feature before dinner. Any food we would eat would first be offered to the deities in the shrine, as they would also need to eat. They were alive and required the attention we gave to ourselves. I would pay incredible detail to the way food would be arranged for the offering.

Early morning before school I would sit in prayer. Each of us had our personal *puja* prayer kit and spent 20 minutes praying and chanting to the images of the gods in front of us. A *puja* prayer kit is a small pouch filled with prints of the various gods that were positioned in the sanctuary of our north London temple. These were to be laid out on a fine piece of cloth with respect and care. The pouch had a rosary within it which you would turn to chant the name of the main deity. After the chanting and meditation on Guruji, we would read the scripture that listed the rules and regulations of our particular denomination. This would remind us daily of our disciplines and boundaries.

Everyone had a personal prayer kit and it would travel with us wherever we went. It was part of the luggage. Like thousands, I would not even take a drop of water in the morning without having a bath, chanting and meditating on the images in this way. Before we did anything for ourselves, we would first do something for God. I took personal care looking after the kit, and ensured that the cloth the images were sat on was neat, clean and well-ironed all the time. When I left home, I took out another rosary from my pocket and began to chant and pray on my way to school.

I was dedicated and committed to serve and worship our Hindu gods and Guruji. Now, I was very serious about my walk, and the other kids in the temple were looking towards me for guidance and inspiration. Matters had turned around in a rapid and serious way. My heart had changed.

I wanted to visit the temple more and more, and began to take part in many activities as well as hosting many at home with my family. My grandfather (my mother's father) would jokingly and with a little concern say, 'Mitesh, you may end up as a *swami*, a priest, if you're not too careful. You're too engrossed, don't you think?'

In my mind I thought, Yes, I'd love to be a *swami*. The idea of spending time with friends and Guruji and enjoying God forever thrilled me. At first this desire to be a *swami* oscillated frequently in my heart. It came and went in a day, just like the British sunshine. But the pattern gradually changed, and the thought of being a *swami* began to take root over the next two years.

The gigantic Townsend Thoresen ferry, *Herald of Free Enterprise*, had just capsized, killing 193 passengers and all the crew. Our family – and others from the temple – had often used it to cross over to Europe with our car, so we were deeply shocked. We were discussing the video footage in detail one Saturday after the temple service. During the chatter, the conversation between us changed and my friends began to talk about life as a *swami*, a priest serving Guruji forever. It was an exciting moment and my heart began to race.

My family often asked me, 'Mitesh, what do you want to do when you grow up?'

I had no idea, except to give the standard Patel answer, 'Doctor, pharmacist or accountant.' Yet I was never quite convinced in my heart, even though it was the traditional thing to do.

Whilst they were mulling over their futures that evening in the temple, one friend, Yogesh, turned to me and said, 'So Mits, you going to join us and be a *swami*?'

The penny dropped. It seemed right. Of course, a group of us close friends departing on a spiritual journey together… I turned to him and said, 'Yes! Definitely! I'm in and I can't wait to start the journey.' In that excitement-filled moment, the thought of being a *swami* was cemented in my heart and was never to change. No matter who said what, I was all in!

Chapter 4
A decision is made

Along with this sudden turn in my life, there were major changes in my home. My mum and dad were increasingly arguing about money and other matters in the household. I never knew who was right or wrong. I just wanted them to stop fighting. We were living in a beautiful five-bedroomed house in a lovely leafy suburb and there were three BMWs in our driveway. Dad had done so well in such a short time, and so I never understood the basis of these intense arguments. I rationalised it all by thinking that these issues and fights must be normal across all my friends' families. In Indian culture, family matters are always protectively kept within the four walls. Outside of that, more often than not, would be a show of glamour, shine and achievement. This aspect is rooted in hiding shame, and so many children never see how other families function through difficult times.

For my parents, the luxury of their life in Kenya, and the knowledge of what they had lost there, must have constantly been on their minds and shaped their behaviour. Of course, I could not understand that at the time. These tensions played a pivotal role in shaping my heart at that age, and I began to look elsewhere for love and a deeper meaning to life. If this was marriage, I didn't want it.

Money, status, class and comparison crippled our family dynamics for years. It's quite sad and yet prevalent in many Indian families. Having a distinguished education, a top home in a classy area, fancy cars and a swanky, exquisite and expensive wedding means that you've justified your existence in society. These are the themes around which our Patel community in general has had strife for many decades.

During this uncomfortable period, my visits to the temple became more frequent. It was now my outlet and space to breathe in peace. I would attend midweek, sweep the floors, wash the utensils or just sit and pray before the images. I began to like it more and more and found it calming and peaceful. I stayed overnight on many weekends to take part in various activities that we would perform during religious festivals. Saturday nights were fun. Friends and I would cook and eat together. We would play football or cricket indoors and then practise speech, drama or dance for any upcoming festival. My reading of the Hindu scriptures began to develop and I started learning verses by heart and could easily quote them mid-conversation. I was fasting quite regularly and decided to sleep on the floor at home to add more simplicity and discipline to my life. I cancelled most TV from my schedule, watching only the news.

The temple Hindu teaching was to decrease everything in one's personal life so that one could connect with God more. If I wanted to please Guruji, I would have to do more for him. The longer my list of disciplines and sacrifice, the more he would be happy. So I fasted from chocolate, cheese, comfy nice clothes and more. The list of things to keep my life very basic and strict continued to grow.

I became more and more desperate to get the attention of Guruji. Our philosophy and theology was fairly straightforward: God spoke and lived through Guruji. Only through him: he was the only vessel pure and capable to carry God. So if he was pleased, so was God. If I wanted to get to heaven and not hell I must never upset him. He was the gateway. He was God on earth.

So at this time, many things made sense. I didn't want to be a doctor or an accountant. I was unhappy with family affairs. Guruji was God and I had his attention. It was very simple and straightforward, and I was set for heavenly success.

With these pieces making sense, my thought-life was focused on one thing: how could I be a *swami*? A priest? And develop a continuous life of this peace and elation that I was feeling with Guruji and at weekends in the temple? This must be the way – the only way – for eternal peace. How could one live in the world and stay so in tune with God? It was impossible, I thought. The hassle of family and wealth would never help me get closer to God and heaven. This was my chance to escape this life and get to heaven. I didn't want to come back to this earth and journey through it again.

These were the consistent thoughts in my mind and the minds of my temple friends with whom I now spent most of my time. When *swamis* came from India we spent our time with them, travelling from home to home holding meetings and praying. Home visits by the *swamis* were a key aspect of their life. It would give them insight into the family affairs and as a result help to guide them if need be. *Swamis* were the route to Guruji for the household members. As a result they were given a lot of respect, honour and trust. In between home visits, these *swamis* sat with us to explain how mundane the worldly life is. There were regular hints and suggestions towards becoming a *swami*. I felt exclusive and special. I was chosen to do this. Living and worshipping with friends: what a life that would be! No hassle, no fighting!

My parents noticed my involvement with the *swamis* and the temple and were becoming more and more concerned. They began to share their worries with close relatives and friends. My time with family and relatives was being heavily sidelined, and my studies began to suffer, too. I missed so many family events. But who cares? I thought. It's worldly and attaching. It's not going to get me to heaven. I was focused and adamant.

Each Hindu has a desire to sit with their god in their respective heaven. Until the soul is purified by service and devotion to the gods and gurus, one has to reincarnate back into earth and finish the task. Each time on earth the soul takes on another body and, based upon its previous spiritual performance, starts at a certain pace of growth. If somebody very quickly gains spiritual growth, that must be because they have done a lot of work in their previous life. The ultimate goal is to stop the cycle of birth and death and sit in heaven. This requires a lot of faith and dedication to a very spiritual lifestyle. I wanted that badly and I would allow nobody to talk me out of it.

In 1988, Guruji came to London for a visit; I was 16. He was 63 at the time and the president and leader of a massive network of followers. He had a unique and special personality; a man of few words, and very gentle. There was something very peaceful and calming about him. I was captivated by this rare and very different person.

One evening, I was asked to speak in the congregation. I was the head of the early teenagers' activities, and so to represent them I had to say something. Guruji was present, along with 3,000 followers. I spoke very well. I was fluent and articulate, not nervous for one second. All the childhood practice paid off. He loved it. Throughout my speech, he acknowledged and agreed to every sentence. I was swept off my feet. The crowd was ecstatic, and went into a cacophony of clapping and cheering as I went towards him to bow. I touched his feet with my forehead in reverence, and looked up into his eyes.

'You are a gifted speaker… you should be a *swami*… you'll make a very good *swami*.' He said these words with sincerity.

That was it. I was overwhelmed and overjoyed. If Guruji says I can be a *swami*, then nothing will prevent it, as that's my calling. I'm designed and destined for this. He knows everything. He is omnipotent and omnipresent – that is what I've learned and heard. He has God inside of him, and soon I'll be on my journey towards a heaven with him.

I remember these thoughts darting across my mind as they brought me a sense of purpose and peace. Guruji's acknowledgement and confirmation of my exclusivity was becoming more and more public, and so my life felt less and less mundane.

My parents were now stuck. My dad had no choice. He was surrendered to Guruji in his own way and so found it difficult to upset him. But he was in checkmate, as my mother was furious at this announcement. In our community, most parents wanted their children to do very well financially, establish a family and then, on weekends, go to the temple. That was as much as they really wanted. Parents loved serving the *swamis* but were very reluctant to let their own child become one. Very few became *swamis* as it had huge consequences on the family lineage. So, though parents were heavily tuned into the temple, equally they didn't want their boys to go over the top!

Looking back, I feel sad for the predicament I placed my dad in. It cannot have been easy. That same evening, though, I had the biggest shock when my brother went to Guruji and asked if he could be a *swami* too! I didn't know of any desire like this on his part. Why didn't he ever tell me? He knew I wanted to become one as well. Why didn't he mention this?

That same year I went with Guruji on a grand tour of the US. I did well in my GSCEs and so my parents gave permission for both my brother and me to travel with him. Both Mum and Dad came to drop us at Gatwick Airport as we left for Miami. I remember my mother at the departures, crying, as we were to leave her for two months. I remember the sadness in her eyes. I could tell she knew what was coming. Mothers are incredibly insightful. Mum didn't say much, but I could see she was hurting. Yet she was beautifully patient, humble and submitting to the whole idea. It was a deep gesture of her silent love for us. She looked at me with a quiet depth. Her eyes said it all: 'Son, you don't know what you're heading into… but I agree, because I love you… please look after yourself.' Dad stood there keeping everything as firm and calm as he could.

'We'll be back soon,' I said. Excited about the plane journey, I turned away and ran to the gate. I do wonder about the heaviness of heart Mum must have gone home with that night. I'm not sure if she even slept.

Chapter 5
Adamant and single-minded

Our Continental Airlines Flight CO31 landed at Miami International Airport. Everything was big. The cars, the roads, the buildings, and especially the food portions! A large 7Up fizzy drink was nearly the size of a bucket, and ridiculously cheap!

Hindus and Gujarati Indians in general were financially thriving by this time in the US. Many, as in the UK, had arrived via East Africa, but most had journeyed directly from India to find a better life. This mass migration to the land of abundant opportunity began largely after the US government initiated the Immigration and Nationality Act in 1965. As anywhere in the world, Gujaratis worked very hard to climb the financial ladder, and the fruits of their hard work were far more evident in the US than in England.

The ownership of motels across America was the biggest and quickest cash cow. It was a lucrative business with very high profit margins. By 2010 nearly one-third of all motels across the US were owned by Gujaratis. Typically, like the newsagents in the UK, the whole family would be involved in the business and, as a result, lead it towards success.

Others who were higher up the education ladder were in various fields of medicine. There was a growing Gujarati community entering into engineering with well-established corporations such as NASA and Boeing. The homes they owned were very large, with beautiful swimming pools. It was a different dimension for me to see this amount of wealth on the other side of the Atlantic. I enjoyed it.

After a day or so we met Guruji, who had just paid a short visit to Trinidad. He welcomed us with the utmost attention. He asked me detailed questions about my journey, where I was staying and how long I'd be with him, along with Raj. I was totally and completely captivated by this man, by everything about him. His hypnotic stare. The way he spoke. The way he ate. The way he met people and conducted the affairs of such a massive and international denomination which we now called an organisation.

Our particular denomination was only 200 years old and had started with very humble beginnings back in Gujarat. It was only in the previous eight years that it had seen a sudden growth internationally. By now Guruji had almost 8,000 centres and temples on nearly every continent. He was the leader and president of nearly a million very dedicated and loyal members. He had captured their hearts in his 40 years of service as president by going to thousands of homes in villages and cities across every nation he visited. At the cost of his health and personal needs, he spent hours of his time with people, listening to their various issues and problems. He took a personal interest in everyone's life and responded to every letter his followers sent him. Somehow, he managed to remember the smallest details, such as food likes or even home addresses. He was a brilliant listener!

The level of dedication Guruji had for his people was quite unprecedented, and so as a result people gave their hearts, minds and money to his cause easily and abundantly. He was gifted in the choice of his words and never disclosed much of what was going on in his heart. When he did, that would be a special moment for the listener. I had the chance to hear matters and questions of his heart frequently, his concerns about certain difficult people who were not listening to his guidance, or the general need for money to complete big temple projects. I was sold, as I was a chosen one from his very inner circle of trustworthy followers from that tender age. Completely bowled over and engulfed, I couldn't believe my luck and destiny as I was handpicked to be in such a close personal place with this man who was God on earth. My excitement knew no bounds as we began our tour across this beautiful country.

Our journey would take us across the US for two months, covering 45,000 miles, visiting small and large cities and reaching out to the Indian community wherever we went. The service or meeting in each town or city would begin with the *swamis* singing Hindu worship songs along with the traditional Indian harmonium (keyboard) and *tabla* (a pair of drums dating back centuries in Indian history). After the worship, a *swami* would give a talk based upon the Hindu scriptures, and then Guruji would speak at the end. The service would finish with very tasty and abundant food. That's normal for Gujaratis. Feeding people and ensuring there is an abundance of food was and still is a main aspect of our culture. Hindus believe in *athiti Devo bhava*. This ancient Sanskrit verse means 'treat your guests as you would treat God'.

Every centre that hosted us made huge preparations for the service, and the most exquisite throne seat for Guruji. He would always be seated on an ornate throne high above everyone else on the stage. This was obvious, as he was God's representation. Nobody questioned it as it was the way we showed our love to him. Cities competed in a healthy way to see who could build the most elaborate and expensive throne.

My duties were to help prepare his private room wherever we travelled. I would make sure it was dark in the room by lining the windows with black dustbin bags so that no sunlight could disturb his rest during the day. I prepared his bed at a tilt, with sheets from the finest Egyptian cotton. Raj and I were chosen to do all his personal buying from that year onwards. In England, we bought Guruji's room needs from Harrods, and in the US from various malls that only sold the best. It was a form of devotion to buy the best for him. What can one not do for God? I washed his clothes with scented water with a blend of 4711 perfume, and helped him put on his shoes made by the British manufacturer Church's. His luggage I would buy from the Italian designer Tumi. Followers would lovingly pay for whatever was needed, and I just had to do the elaborate shopping, which was a fun experience as it gave me a lot of exposure to brands and the world of luxury. Only a handful would be able to serve him food, help him up the stairs, sit next to him on the plane or beside him in his car. I was always his first choice and nobody would challenge that, even though there were hints of jealousy. I had a position in his heart and schedule that anybody would die for.

Guruji had a full team of servants to attend to him wherever he went in the world. A secretary for his letters and phone calls. A head of logistics and travel. A cook. A reporter who would write every detail of his day, and two full-time servants to aid him with bathing and other things. It was like a mobile political campaign. This team were all ordained *swamis*. They had spent years in the organisation, training and learning. I was 16 and I had the same access to Guruji as they had! I was allowed access to his room regardless of the privacy of the meeting. Whether the meeting involved financial matters or crucial global decisions, I was never stopped. Suddenly, internationally I was known as his chosen one, a 'favourite'.

I still have no idea why I was given so much so soon. What senior *swamis* said to me then was that I had an abundance of 'good deeds' accumulated from my past lives which must be the only reason for so much affection from Guruji. Many lifetimes of hard spiritual work must now have come to fruition.

'Mitesh, there are *swamis* who were ordained by him 30 years ago who have given their whole and total life to him, and yet Guruji doesn't know their name! As for you, he knows your every move and mood.' I found that strange as I thought, He knows everything about everyone. Anyhow, I was chuffed!

During these months in the USA, Guruji began to talk to me about the future and his purpose for me, the areas where he wanted me to be and to succeed. 'Start speaking in public,' he would say. 'Get as much practice as you can from now on.' He had seen me speak and, like my schoolteachers, knew there was something very easy about the way I did it.

Once, in New Jersey, Guruji and I were sitting alone in his room. He had finished writing his letters, and turned to me with a soft and gentle smile. 'When you come on this side as a *swami*, you may notice certain strange things. This will lead you to many questions. Try not to ponder too much. Stay focused on me.'

I sat there wondering what he meant by this, yet passive as I knew he would protect and guide me if ever I came across any tight corners in the future. I was feeling protected, and I truly was.

Day after day that confirmation came through. At one stage in Chicago, the CEO of the USA region approached me and said, 'You cannot hang around here for too long. You'll have to go back to London as we don't have space in every town and city for such a large group.' I was sad, yet felt sure that I'd have to leave. He had been the CEO for 30 years in the USA, Guruji's right-hand man for growth in the nation, and a very close confidant. He was very respected by the whole congregation and managed to raise millions of dollars for Guruji's work in India.

'Sure,' I said.

That evening, Guruji was told by one of his attendants that I was leaving, going back to the UK. He immediately called the CEO and said, 'Mitesh will stay with me all the way. Nobody will send him anywhere! He will join my entourage wherever it goes in the US!' The CEO asked no questions and immediately agreed. When I heard this, I was flabbergasted. Such a stern and overriding decision. Guruji rarely intervened with local decisions, especially about a 16-year-old and whether he could stay or go back to London! Overnight the whole of the USA management realised that they were to stay very clear of me.

That night, as I went with a group of friends to see the Chicago skyline and the super-tall Sears Tower, as it was then called, I thought over the whole scene. I walked beside Lake Michigan, admiring the beautiful skyline made by man and the lake made by God. Wondering with elation, I believed in the most ecstatic future ahead of me.

On one occasion during the evening service in Atlanta, Guruji turned and looked at me in the midst of his speech. Thousands were seated before him. He smiled and said, 'I have trust that this boy will one day perform great things for our organisation. He will advance it in many ways.' The crowd looked to see who he was talking about, and suddenly I was the centre of attention. I had just come back from visiting the big Coca-Cola factory and so my mind was a little caffeinated already; now that statement heightened the buzz. I was convinced that my destiny was to do great works for him and the organisation. I could see the pieces being put in place, and people began to look after me with incredible attention to detail.

This extraordinary acknowledgement was attracting a lot of attention. It led to some tricky challenges that I never knew existed in what I thought was an almost utopian environment. People battled for my full attention and support. Very early during that US tour I noticed cracks among the *swamis* which led to some trouble in my mind. I saw the struggle for position and power. The life of a *swami* was totally dependent on Guruji and the organisation's trustees and senior *swamis*. To progress in your career, you had to have support and favour from this very small handful of decision-makers. However, to make life easy, if you had access to the very top, which was Guruji, it then became very difficult for the other people in power to have any impact on your work, role or responsibility. This fear of losing control of your future to 'interference' from the authorities higher up in the hierarchy led to *swamis* competing and playing very sharp elbow politics.

I had a rough idea of the chessboard and how things were being played. Whoever was close to Guruji and had his attention had a greater authority and command over friends, and over appointments of position and finance. You had great measures of independence that nobody could challenge but Guruji. It became very difficult for anyone else to complain about you when you had the ear of the person they complained to!

Guruji's reporter had written stories for the archives of how I had his ear, attention, support and ridiculous favour. Very quickly mine became a household name within the organisation, and so now *swamis* wanted my attention and began to bicker for it.

Guruji found out that I was troubled and immediately set aside everything to attend to me privately. His PA came to search for me one afternoon whilst we were in New York.

'Mitesh, Guruji is calling you,' I heard a voice say. Immediately I sprang up, climbed the stairs and entered his room. He was writing letters so I waited a few minutes in the silence of his presence. Nobody else was in the room. He folded away his reading glasses and focused all his attention on me in one look.

'What's wrong?'

I narrated various incidents of *swamis* bickering and arguing. I asked him why they were fighting for my attention, as I found it so strange. 'Why is power and position such a big thing here, when you are the face and mouth of God? It doesn't add up!' I said.

He listened very attentively, which was one of his remarkable gifts. He then spoke in a soft and reassuring voice. 'Now, I told you earlier on. Stay focused on me. Always remember, the guru is faultless and flawless. So calm down and be at peace. You're here for me and nobody else. If anybody hassles you from now on, just tell me and I'll talk to them. These things happen, as it's human nature. People have issues, and so try not to let it trouble you.'

He finished what he had to say and became silent. The silence meant that I was to get up and leave. As I left the room I felt much better but a little uncomfortable. The flag was raised and the battle in my mind had begun. Guruji was God and my gateway to heaven. I knew that firmly. Yet why were matters around him such a mess? Surely after spending years as a *swami* there would be change.

I was naïve, of course, and I don't know if I was any different from the others in wanting to be attached to Guruji and enjoy his favour. It was natural, too, that a 'favourite' would attract jealousy. Anyway, after that day I realised that it was imperative to stay close to Guruji and have his support in all matters.

Two months of serving, travel and fun passed quickly. I had the privilege of seeing most of America, and gained an incredible insight into the culture and lifestyle of that vast land at various levels. I never knew then, but the benefit of travelling extensively would continue for years to come, and with it, a God that I didn't know yet. A God that I didn't know existed. A God who was hidden from me by some sort of veil would continue to push the boundaries and borders ingrained in my early thought-life to challenge me continuously.

Chapter 6
No return

Raj and I departed with heavy hearts. Guruji told me on our departure, 'Phone me whenever you want. I've told my secretary always to pass your call straight through to me.' I was glad of that. We took our return flight from Dallas Fort Worth airport. Our aircraft was a DC-10 TriStar, probably the last of those around, I thought.

We arrived back in London on a dark and cloudy day. Mum and Dad had come to collect us from London's Gatwick Airport. There was a disturbing silence in the car as they drove us home. An hour of silence can feel like an eternity when there's a lot of discomfort in the air. No words, no questions. It was eerie. Things had changed drastically both in me and in them. From that day, my relationship with my parents deteriorated rapidly. I began to limit my communication with them, and things at home became very formal. I became very silent and dissociated internally, as now in my heart my mum and dad was Guruji!

I knew what was racing through their minds. Our child must not leave to be a *swami*. But my mind was clear. I'll do whatever it takes. Raj was of the same view, and so this common goal bonded my brother and me for the next few years as never before. We spent more and more time with each other.

Wherever we went or whatever we did, it would be together. His friends were my friends. I had just started my A levels and he was pursuing his degree in accountancy. The pressure at home was now manageable, as he was there beside me.

At school a lot had changed, too. I disconnected with many of my friends and teachers. My maths teacher, Ms Matthews, once quietly took me aside after class and asked, 'Are you OK?'

'Fine,' I replied.

She continued, 'I'm not happy with the change in you. You used to be such a happy guy, mixing and having fun with everyone. You're now doing your A levels and we really have high hopes for you to go to a top university. You're one of our finest students, and so we need you to focus.'

She was genuinely concerned, I could see, but at that time I brushed it aside, thinking that it was a distraction to my destiny. We were taught by the *swamis* that as you take this path many distractions will come from *maya*, the Hindu demon of dark illusion.

The term *maya* is prevalent across all the Hindu denominations as an equal to the devil. It's the multifaceted lure of deception. This evil force plays with your mind in a variety of ways through lust, greed or even negative words of distraction from the path to that particular heaven you wish to reach. This theory kept me more and more intense about ignoring anyone and everyone who tried to love me out of this idea. My rugby trainer, Mr Wilson, asked if I would continue playing for the team but I was not interested. Whoever came in my way now was *maya*. A distraction between me and heaven!

This was the mindset and attitude that etched itself deeper as the weeks at home and school went by. A girl called Annabelle had been in my class for years and we had had several dates in the past. She came and sat by me and said that she would love to nominate me as head boy for the school. I had been head of the third year and so friends and teachers wanted me to continue in a similar capacity. I was completely uninterested. I turned to her and said, 'If I win, I'll decline.'

I remember Annabelle's expectant, joyous face suddenly turning to disappointment. 'What's the matter with you?' her kind face suggested. I stood up and left the classroom. Another distraction, I thought. In this way I stopped my schoolfriends, teachers and family from loving me. I was so focused on my future that I did not care for anything and anyone any more.

In 1991, the First Gulf War was coming to an end. In my home there was an ongoing war of a different kind. I was getting restless about my future and the time had come to leave for priesthood. To be a *swami!* The organisation had a policy that you had to have written consent from parents and be aged above 19. The latter wasn't a problem, but the former really was. We debated endlessly at home about this, but my parents just would not sign the document of consent.

To leave and be a *swami* meant complete renunciation, otherwise known in Sanskrit as *tyagi*, and that would mean I could no longer communicate with my parents or have any ties with my background or childhood. I would not be able to marry, and so I'd have no family to continue the family lineage my parents were so proud of. Hence, for them it was a stab in the heart.

Friends and family tried to explain to me how difficult it was for my parents to give away two boys, but I was just not ready to listen. 'No!' I would say. 'This is all a distraction from my destiny!'

As I write this, I do wonder. What was I thinking? What happened to me? What came over me to ignore the love of friends and family? All my reasoning had departed, and all that was left was this narrow mindset to serve God and guru with this life. I was special. I had been selected. I had been chosen to do great things! My stubbornness, combined with my pride at this glorious destiny, blocked out everything else.

My parents sent many friends to try to talk me out of this but I turned them all away. Even though my mum and dad were dedicated followers of the temple, they somehow felt that there were some aspects that were not right at all, or healthy.

There are many admirable qualities in our Gujarati tradition, with its emphasis on spirituality and discipline. But one struggle, in my opinion, is that people at times can appear to follow their faith quite passively. By this I mean they would rather not address any major issues they are not comfortable with. The reason, I've noticed, is that if they ask too many questions about the faith, its morals, ethics or general attitude and approach to finance and people, then they would be blacklisted. This would subdue any further 'growth' in terms of roles or responsibility within the temple activities. They would not get easy access to key people or places within the structure. The quicker and more readily you agree to what the hierarchical system says, the easier it is for you to be recognised, loved and accepted.

My parents knew that this whole issue would be a huge tension zone for them. On one side it was us, their children, and on the other was the loss of face within the organisation if they stopped us. Many sympathised with them, but as Guruji was on my side, it was safer for those friends to stay quiet. I ignored all advice and help and stayed firm, always believing that there's a cost to getting to heaven!

At this time I had a conversation with Guruji and informed him that my parents were not giving consent. He suggested that Raj and I wait for a while, and if my parents still paid no heed, we were to give them a warning and just leave. That was astounding! Guruji went against the organisation's policy of written consent to have me on his team. I was wonderstruck at what he was prepared to do in order to have me. Senior *swamis* and trustees questioned him on this decision. His reply to them was simple: 'Stay out of this. I'm handling it.' After that, everybody at the very senior level in India and the UK stayed quiet and took a back seat. Nobody interfered from that day on in any of my affairs.

Finally, after much debate, I gave my parents a warning that we would leave if they were not willing to sign the document. They still didn't budge, and we began to plan for our departure.

We prepared with clinical precision. Nobody knew what was going on except for a handful of friends. I didn't tell Guruji the date of departure. In that way he would not get any blame or have to lie, as we were sure that as soon as my parents knew, he would be the first port of call. If he didn't know where we were or when we had left, he would be left alone. With the utmost stealth, day by day we bought and collected clothes and hid them in a bag which remained in my friend's car. This way our cupboards wouldn't look so empty. We bought airline tickets with Emirates airlines. The tickets were posted to my friend Hiren and not to us. We decided to fly from Gatwick as Heathrow was an airport where we might see familiar faces, and so it wasn't worth the risk. We wanted to ensure a breather of a few days before anybody could find out. Before the morning of departure, we began to spend a lot of time away from home. For weeks we began a rhythm of being gone for the day with friends or just resting at the temple. This way, when the day of leaving arrived, it would look like just another normal day out. But this time, it would be to Mumbai!

It was a Friday – 25th October 1991. Cloudy and windy. We had no luggage. Our prayer kits had already been placed in my friend's car the night before, and that morning we used an alternative one. You can see the planning behind our run. It was precise and foolproof.

My dad came out of the bathroom as we were leaving. 'You're early today?'

I didn't expect him to ask that. Did he know? My heart started beating fast and the first thing that came to my mind was, 'Eh, we are going shopping all day. Lots to buy!'

He looked at me with a concerned face. He didn't push any further. I don't completely know, but I have a feeling now that my dad knew where we were really going that Friday morning. Mum was still fast asleep. I feel he let it happen. That's my dad. A man of grace and utmost patience. He gave me £10 for my travel. I still have no idea why he did that. We both had plenty of money at all times. But he gave extra that morning. I feel he alone knows the reason as to why he did that.

We left our home for the last time on that cloudy morning. My favourite home of all time, situated on a hill. My window with the beautiful view of planes landing miles away at Heathrow, and the church situated next to Harrow School. I loved my home: my lovely blue bedroom, my cosy bed, my desk.

The roads in our area were lined with beautiful houses and tall trees which always brought joy to my walk to school. Today's walk was different. It was to the next street where two of our friends, Amish and Sameer, were waiting in the getaway car. They had hired a red Volkswagen Golf. We left the house looking as casual as we could, but my heart was racing. The slightest hitch and there would be an explosion. I chanted the guru's name for protection until we got to the car. I saw the faces of Amish and Sameer who were just as scared as we were. If they were found to have helped us in this, the whole congregation would be on them like a ton of bricks. This was a lifetime secret. After we were gone, they had to lie to hundreds of people and pretend that they hadn't the foggiest idea about us.

We sat in the car and finally took a deep breath. We laughed, joked and then panicked. Only once we were in the air would we be totally home and dry. We raced off to Gatwick Airport, constantly looking in the rear-view mirror to ensure my dad wasn't following in his golden BMW. On arrival, another group of friends who were in on the plan met us, and we all sat and promised each other to keep this a secret. We had a brief chat and they brought me my favourite Sky ice cream. I looked around at their faces. A few would be joining us on the journey of becoming a *swami* later, but the others were taking a different path, the 'normal' path. This separate walk meant a lot of separation at many levels with some of my friends.

It was slowly dawning on me that this was real and hard. I showed a defiant face, however, and just then our boarding sign came up. We looked at each other. Sameer, Amish, Jayesh, Vikesh and Priyam, all of us suddenly nervous. At that point, Vikesh turned to me and said, 'Have no regrets, dear friend. None.'

I felt he knew a little more than I did about the 'other side' – life as a *swami*. I was a little shaken by that. He repeated again, 'Remember, no regrets.' My heart rate went up, but I still held on to my bold face.

We said our goodbyes and gave our hugs. Heavy-hearted, with my destiny in view, I walked towards the gate and we boarded our flight. I did feel a pang of separation that day. A very deep one. But I hid my emotions fairly well. This was my first conscious attempt at hardening my heart. From now, I knew that emotions must be kept at bay. I mustn't access my pain but hide it at all times. Priesthood was a serious matter.

We boarded the flight, and as the plane took off, I couldn't help but think that my parents were at home going about their normal day, assuming we would be home that evening for dinner. That thought unsettled me and tugged at my heart for some time as I stared over the clouds that hid London from my eyes. Would I ever see this land again? No idea.

I have looked back upon that day and pondered over many thoughts. What if I hadn't run away? What if I had stayed and pursued a normal career instead? Where would my life be now? Again, no idea.

Chapter 7
Training and battles

We arrived in the sunny, sticky and ear-pounding land of India, what I've always kindly called an 'organised chaos'! As I stepped out of the airport, I found that everyone in this complex and fast-living city of Mumbai seemed to know what they were doing except for me. How I would survive in this land I hadn't a clue.

India is a vast and complex country. If anyone today were to ask me for an insight into that rich and ancient land, I wouldn't have any idea where to start and what to include. Before the existing political map with its 29 states and seven union territories, India was an array of hundreds of kingdoms ruled by kings and queens who were always trying to strike alliances with each other or otherwise fight each other. Each state today has an assortment of different cuisines in its regions, as well as different dialects and habits of running a household. You can travel only 30 miles from one village to another in Gujarat and notice a significant difference in the dialect and cuisine. The caste system is still very strong in India. Everybody knows what it is, and everybody explains it differently, because it really is complex! Its influence still has a hold to a certain degree on those who have migrated westwards. There are different castes among the Patels as well, which traditionally would direct you to whom you could or couldn't marry.

Today India hosts the second largest number of people in the world after China, with 22 official languages and more than 1,600 other languages and dialects. Its history is closely tied to the Mughal invasion in the fourteenth century and later, in the seventeenth century, to the British East India Company, which by the 1850s had become the ruling entity over most of its landmass. India hosts all the major world religions. Jews and Christians have been there for at least 1,700 years, and Hinduism, Buddhism, Sikhism and Jainism were birthed there. It has the third largest population of Muslims after Indonesia and Pakistan. It has a democratic government but still struggles with corruption within its political corridors.

After a little rest we had some fun time chilling and eating in the luxurious Taj hotel right opposite the Gateway of India which was built to commemorate the visit of King George V and Queen Mary of Great Britain. We enjoyed the comfort of the sofas and views of the Arabian Sea.

Then we wandered along the Mumbai coastline and tried our best to blend in with the Bollywood swagger. After looking at the hip and trendy Mumbai people, Raj and I realised that we just weren't cool enough! We hadn't watched enough Bollywood movies to really get to grips with being stylish in the Indian way. Bollywood culture is India's biggest influence, a bridge or a common language that all Indians, regardless of their faith or language background, are attuned to. That includes the majority of Indians living in the West as well.

A day and a half into our fantasy tour of this buzzing city, the bomb fell back in London. After endless searching, my parents realised what had actually happened. Through friends I found out that there were countless phone calls being made to and from London, to the USA and to Guruji. It had all kicked off. Globally, we were at the centre of every conversation and gossip within the organisation. Not quite the attention I was hoping for!

Thankfully, Guruji held his ground. He was firm and said that we had the power to make our own choices in life. So my parents and the trustees in London were helpless and eventually had to calm down.

It's important to note here that Guruji had the final say in any matter. If anybody questioned him in anything, then they were questioning God and the results of that would have drastic consequences, both spiritually and socially. This, however tough the situation, was something my parents or the trustees were not willing to do, although I knew how uncomfortable this was for them. You could only suggest or request to a certain point on any matter to Guruji, and then the final choice must always be left to him. This was scripturally founded and widely accepted if you didn't want to go to hell.

It was a huge relief for me that he took our side and didn't send us back. After the rubble was cleared with my parents with awkward phone conversations and hurtful comments, we joined Guruji for a brief tour around the villages of Gujarat from the beginning of November, ending at the training monastery by mid-December.

Gujarat state hosts over 60 million people within its 18,000 villages and many industrial towns and cities. It has a diversity of landscape from deserts to lush green countryside, growing many products from cotton to vegetables and tobacco. It is home to one of the largest oil refineries in the world and has an incredible history dating back centuries with traders from Greece, Egypt and Portugal's Vasco da Gama.

Road journeys can be very bumpy and jerky with plenty of potholes and cows strolling in the middle of the road. Seat belts are not compulsory, and frankly there are no normal road rules. It's something you get used to after a brief spout of frustration. Car horns are frequently used to tell people that you are passing through a village or crowded city area. The clamour of many car horns continues late into the night and begins again in the early morning. Again, it's something you begin to get acquainted with. The gutter system is quite basic and so the smell can be pungent and almost suffocating at times. People use the side of the roads as their WC and are humorously fine with it.

England was far away now and all I heard about my favourite land was that Tesco and Asda had just decided to open on Sundays to beat the ongoing recession. The recession had been a major issue in 1991. Many Gujaratis had placed a lot of money in the Bank of Credit and Commerce International (BCCI), which collapsed that year with millions of pounds belonging to the Gujarati community in London. What happened to the British or US economy mattered to Guruji very much, as these were the nations providing millions of pounds and dollars to build his beautiful marble temples. So we prayed a lot during our travels for the UK economy to come alive.

During my very first week of travel I encountered my first ever tangible experience of a 'silent voice' speaking into my left ear. It was like a piercing knife that placed a doubt into my mind. 'Are you sure you've done the right thing?'

I was rattled by this and tried to shake it off, assuming it was *maya*, the demon of illusion, again. It felt new, as I had never encountered such a thing. Two days later I fell sick with malaria, and so the same doubt had more time in my stillness to speak further into my heart and mind. I kept fighting it, thinking that it was a demon, but the challenge was that the voice seemed rather authentic and genuine. Have you ever been so focused on something, and just then a genuine friend asks you the most profound question which stops you completely in your tracks? That's how I felt, but I didn't know where or who the voice was, so I kept second-guessing it as a demon.

Just then, another *swami* who was helping me in my illness spoke my mind. He sat beside my bed and said, 'Look, Mits, doubts will arise. Don't worry. We are chosen by God himself in Guruji and we are on the right path. These thoughts will come and go. The quicker you learn to ignore them, the faster you will grow.' He mentioned that it happened to everyone and that it was normal.

I sat there pondering his words. It made sense to me that doubts are always a part of life when tough decisions are made. I thought that if everyone suffered from these thoughts then there must be somebody such as Guruji who had the right answer. I concluded that as I matured spiritually through meditation, I would still my mind. By chanting the various names of our Hindu gods and studying the ancient scriptural texts, my mind would come to rest and the doubts would vanish. I was fooling myself.

Raj didn't mention anything to me about doubts or questions, and so I didn't think it was wise to tell him mine. It would worry him if I did, and I didn't want to plant any doubts in him. The number of people, friends and activities on tour helped me stay distracted during these itchy moments. But the minute I spent time alone, my mind would enter a storm of questions and doubts.

Why didn't I just pack up and go back home? First of all I thought it was just a short and simple battle of the mind that would eventually come to rest. This aspect of an initial battle was taught to us by the *swamis* when they had passed through London years before. The teaching about the mind by many Hindu faiths, including mine at the time, was that the mind is like a monkey and never sits still. It's like the wind which blows one way at one moment and then the other the next. So it's never to be trusted and always to be ignored.

Looking back at this teaching, I would say that it disallowed healthy intuition and discretional thinking to be explored – even though it might sound right or sensible philosophically. Thus I kissed my brain goodbye and allowed this kind of teaching to manipulate my inner life. Years later I would understand how this theology was rooted in control and fear. At the time I had no other idea.

But more than this, the world congregation knew that I was meant for a special cause, and so did I. I had just run away from home to prove my passion for my destiny, and now if I went back, the shame and guilt would be overbearing. Indian culture in general, regardless of faith background, has a lot of relationships that largely perform out of guilt and shame, especially if anyone in the family does not perform to certain expectations.

My parents and extended family were very upset by my departure and so my return home would tempt them to take even more control over my life by reiterating how wrong I was. This was culturally normal to them. My response to live and continue out of fear was equally typically cultural.

In addition, I was in the spotlight, destined for many great things, and so I couldn't afford to sadden Guruji. He had invested his time and energy in me like no other. He had stood his ground to back me and spent hours speaking into my life and catering for my smallest needs. So Guruji, my parents, my friends and even the global congregation who knew about this 'famous and chosen Mitesh' were very difficult to upset and let down.

So, in the middle of these thought-provoking challenges, I kept forcing my mind to believe that it was a battle against my destiny, which I did partly believe. I pushed on, thinking of different ways to suppress the thoughts and be at peace.

We arrived with Guruji at the training monastery and spent some time near him before our training began. I spent a lot of time in his room, cleaning and preparing his bed and bathroom. I helped with his letters when his secretary went for lunch or dinner. I read out the letters sent to him in English and translated them for him. I was nervous that he was to leave after a month and that my actual journey would now begin. I was so dependent on Guruji and reliant on his proximity that time without him was daunting. I was still having shaky moments but I tried to keep them to myself. I had realised how much I had come against to get here, so a sign that I was crumbling would completely shock everyone.

At one time I was attending the evening corporate worship in the temple. Suddenly I felt my heart race and vividly remember stopping myself from bowing to the images, and going to look over the balcony. In that moment, a silent voice with a deep sense of concern spoke again and said, 'What are you doing here? You're not supposed to be here. You're in the wrong place.'

It was like an earthquake. I lost all emotional balance. I kept staring over the balcony and lost all sense of the worship and people around me. The temple floor was packed with at least 100 other *swamis* fully engaged in singing and clapping. The bells and drums were still playing hard and yet I felt suddenly strange and isolated, scared and disconnected. My heart began to race further, and for a brief few moments nothing around me made sense.

After that, the still small voice continued to stay with me and ask questions with the utmost honesty and sincerity. If and when it spoke I struggled to battle with its integrity, and so I began to pretend that it was just my mind playing up, to pretend that it never spoke, to pretend that it was all fine, another *maya* moment.

From that day in the temple worship, this hiding and covering of the truth edged me to a very shiny, cosmetic and pretentious lifestyle. I got so good at pretending that I could even pretend to myself. My life of two worlds had begun. An inner one of growing disbelief, although trying my best to believe, and the other, an outer showing of a brave face that all was well and fine.

In January 1992, Guruji finally left the monastery, and a month later training began with a mixture of intense moments and emotions. The training centre was an oasis in the middle of the desert in Gujarat. Although a desert, the monastery leaders had learned a few ingenious techniques from Israeli farmers and their drip irrigation system which enabled us to grow some very helpful products. We had 250 acres of land enriched with cotton fields, pomegranate trees, orange groves, mango groves and even watermelons. We sold a lot of our products at a very good price which helped to sustain the upkeep of the temple, its campus and 150 *swamis* and students like me. There were always donations arriving from overseas so there was never any lack.

The training centre was built around a 100-year-old temple that Guruji's teacher had built. The quietness, solitude and land space allowed it to develop into a university-type campus filled with classrooms and dormitory-type residences. It was very impressive and beautiful. Certain aspects about the Indian landscape are very attractive. From the dorm room I lived in I could see the beautiful sunset and the fields of pomegranate trees.

The diverse colours of the Indian sun throughout the day are unique. As the sun set in the west, radiating its bronze colour, I would wonder secretly what was happening in my homeland of England. From the brief news we acquired from the very rare phone calls, all we knew was that the Football Association was creating a new Premier League to begin that same year. Completely different issues from the rampant Hindu–Muslim riots that were taking place in various cities around India.

I never knew the issue was so deep and dated until I arrived there. Hindus and Muslims had been fighting and killing each other for centuries, and now it dawned on me that I was almost on the front line to support any pro-Hindu cause. I just wanted to pursue a peaceful, godly life with Guruji.

Anyway, the thorough curriculum and busy timetables of studying and training got me happily distracted. My desk looked very quaint, lined with ancient Hindu scriptures along with notepads. My dorm room was full of others from overseas: USA, Africa and the UK. 'I'm finally here,' I remember saying. There was a mix of elation in the midst of my questions as the buzz of more than 100 other trainees helped to drown out my doubts and worries.

The training years from 1992 to 1995 were to develop a life of discipline and order, both mental and physical. 'Simple living and high thinking' was the general theme. This began with me having to sleep in the same dorm hall as everyone and eat with everyone at the same time allocated. No activity from now on was in private except the time I was in the lavatory! I enjoyed the community life. Every day was full of activity and study. Large groups moving from class to class or from the main hall to the campus temple. Yoga classes here or music groups there. Any form of exercise was encouraged, whether yoga or a run around the campus. Fitness and discipline of the body helped the sharpness of the mind. It was a very vibrant and diverse group of people taking a deep interest in either cooking or learning how to play classical Indian instruments such as *tabla* or the stringed sitar.

I acknowledged in these early days that no possession was to be privately mine. I owned nothing. I now belonged to the organisation, dedicated and committed to do as they said. Personal lifestyle had vanished forever: no bank account, no money. I could not even touch money!

There was a very extreme view of greed as a priest in our particular denomination, and so any temptation of its arousal was clamped down with strict rules and discipline. Some Hindu denominations allow their priests or *swamis* to have money, but Guruji didn't want this. He felt that private and personal money would lead to secret agendas and *swamis* would then go astray. Money would bring freedom and he didn't want that. He wanted complete dependency and trust that we would be provided for. This, of course, would enable the members of the congregation to keep trust in us when we were preaching about values, simplicity and the downfall of false habits such as greed. Raising money would be easy too, as members would acknowledge that none of the money would go into personal accounts.

However, later on in my journey I found out that some *swamis* did manage to create personal bank accounts and were privately investing in homes and the like, just in case they decided to leave abruptly. Most of the time when these *swamis* were caught out, they were asked to leave. However, if it turned out to be a senior *swami* engaged in such matters, it would be swept under the carpet and not mentioned at all, as this would be such an embarrassment to Guruji. I was told by Guruji that this was not corruption but the downside of human behaviour, and thus it shouldn't bug me. It did bug me. How could this take place in the house of God?

I was dependent on the organisation from now on. If I needed anything or wanted to leave the building for any reason, I would have to inform the respective *swami* in charge of that particular temple. The commitment now was that I was never to be out of sight or alone at any single moment in my life. Wherever I travelled, even a short walk, I would have the company of others. They would pay for anything I might need, and understandably the cost would be registered. My life was not my own now, but I was fully committed to the organisation and its people, always surrounded and monitored. I knew that provision would not be an issue as I had seen the vast amount of wealth flowing around, and I was deeply connected to Guruji as well.

On one occasion the head mentor approached me and asked, 'Are you OK? Do you need anything?'

I was surprised. 'What? I'm OK. Why?'

'Well, I just came back from a meeting with Guruji, and as I left he was asking about you. He told me to personally take care of any of your needs.'

I was moved. The thought that Guruji was thinking of me in the middle of an international meeting led my affection for him to deeper levels. These countless moments of his commitment to my welfare helped me plough on amidst my questions and doubts.

Chapter 8
Disciplining the senses

By this time my clothes were no longer civilian, but I wore a white *dhoti* and a simple white shirt. White is a common theme in dress code for Hindu priests, as it symbolises purity. At the end of my training I would be ordained into orange clothes, symbolising fire and sacrifice. A *dhoti* is a very long white cloth which somehow had to stay upon my waist without a zip or button! It was more than a different task to the jeans and sweaters I was used to. In fact, it was horrendous.

'How do you wrap this thing around you so it stays up?' I asked Raj one evening. 'It keeps getting loose as the day passes!'

He laughed and said, 'Bro, you don't want that thing falling off in the middle of worship! It may attract attention.'

I panicked and wore it as tight as I could. One morning, though, I woke up when all the others were already in quiet prayer. I was late! But as I rushed to the cupboard to fetch my things, I realised my *dhoti* was still on the mattress! The whole foreign team stared at me and laughed so loud that the silence was broken throughout the whole top floor.

I laughed at myself standing there with only my top on! Ready to walk downstairs for corporate worship and make a complete fool of myself. Many were these moments.

I finally 'styled' my *dhoti* well and it began to stay with me wherever I went. Thus, fun moments were intertwined in my day along with friends who could have a good laugh at anything.

Fasting was very difficult in the Indian climate. I was told that five fasts a month was basic. If that was basic I didn't want to know the advanced level! Each fast meant 36 hours without food or water. Fasting was a way to still the body and disconnect with it. Many Hindu denominations believe that the body gets in the way with its fleshy instincts, and so it must be put to rest by punishment to elevate the soul with prayer, worship and meditation. The soul is what needs to get to heaven. It needs refining and elevation. It's surrounded by evil instincts attached in the flesh and so cannot experience its sublime state without a very deep inner separation with the body.

For a breakthrough in this transition, a guru who has the ultimate elevated soul and who is in constant communion with God is imperative. His insight, guidance and blessing take one to God in heaven, and as we meditate on the guru and his teachings, our soul finds its sublime and serene state here on earth. He is the conduit, and without him there is no way. You cannot go to God directly.

Fasting was a nightmare for me. I couldn't sleep at night because of the intense heat of the tiles beneath my mattress burning through, and my day went by as if I had just run several marathons. One morning, as I was exhausted I broke down into tears. 'How will I make this?' I thought. It became more and more tough as the summers peaked; 40 degrees Celsius was a lot of sunshine!

One day, a group of us decided after much thought to break the fast. We went to the kitchen where the lemons, honey and sugar were stored to make the typical 'Indian lemon drink'. A lemon drink always settles and prepares the stomach before eating after any fast. It's a common drink across India and very cheap to make. Most who live in the villages will offer this drink to guests and friends as it is easy to prepare.

As we approached the kitchen, to my shock there was a padlock on the door. I stood there staring at this lock for a few seconds, as it sent off a very eerie signal. It was a very simple yet eye-opening moment for me. The freedom of choice was not available in this place. The drink that would quench my thirst was on the other side of that locked door. Events like these always stood out like a brick wall as they contradicted the teaching of compassion. However, we ignored such events and found other ways to feed our needs.

I woke up every morning at 4.45 to take a bath. I bathed with cold water as was encouraged, as this was another way to disallow my body its needs. There was the option of hot water but only one tap supplied it, in front of which always stood a queue of elderly *swamis*. I was usually late in the mornings and so I couldn't wait too long and besides, standing in line for hot water just wasn't cool or spiritual. I could get a weird look like, 'What's wrong with you?'

My personal prayer time with my own prayer kit took 45 minutes and then I would run up the stairs to the main temple for corporate *arti* at 6am. I just about made it each time, half-awake and always unable to connect. *Arti* or corporate worship is when we would light lamps and wave them in front of the images. This ritual exists across all the Hindu religions. The belief behind it is for the godly power and spirit of the deities to be infused into the flame as the priest in the inner sanctuary waves it with adoration. After the worship song is over, that flame is passed around to everyone present. I would touch the very top of the flame with my hands and then touch my forehead with respect as a sign to acknowledge that godly spirit and power to come into my soul. Until the flame came to me I would bow and prostrate to the images throughout the worship song, which would take 20 minutes. That's a lot of exercise!

Arti would take place five times a day, and I had to attend at least three. The whole campus was empty during this period as it was a key time to worship together. If I was late or missing it would be noted. It was not a habit I wanted to make, but it was obvious in those days that I just couldn't connect with the various images and gods during these times. I would try harder by singing louder or by fully placing my focus on the images to get some stillness or tranquillity. I felt nothing. Each time I came down the steps from the temple I realised that I had just ticked a box in my head to make myself feel good. But I continued, as did everyone. It was important to keep the rules and do all that was required. There was also the fear of displeasing Guruji.

So I kept on. I didn't tell anyone that I couldn't connect as they would consider me some sort of weird, unspiritual freak. Everybody else, it seemed, was having such an engaging time in a *swami*'s most significant part of the day – except me.

Daily chores took at least one and a half hours. These chores would vary from sweeping the floor to cleaning the toilets. Every 14 days the rota would change. I had to fit this part of my day in between my classes and homework. The quality of my cleaning was checked regularly and if it wasn't up to par I had to do it again.

Sunday was the day of chores only, with no classes or study. A list would be read out in the morning and we would separate into small groups to complete different tasks. This way we managed the upkeep of the whole campus.

One Sunday we were asked to shift marble slabs from one end of the field to the other, and then the next Sunday back to their original place. After four weeks of repetition, I asked a teacher, 'Why don't we decide which corner of the field we want the slabs? Moving them around seems senseless and wastes a lot of time!'

He looked at me and said, 'Exactly! The idea is to break that feeling of "sense" that you have from your upbringing and education, and align it with the teachings of scripture and what Guruji says.'

Hindu thought behind these chores or *seva* (service) is an act to keep one humble and cleanse one of thoughts such as lust, anger, pride or greed. I took on this challenge knowing the depth of my instincts regarding lust and anger. My outbursts of irritation were incredible. I desperately wanted to get rid of them as they were hindering me, and as a result I couldn't focus. I knew from the teaching that if they were not removed by my hard work I would not go to heaven. So I worked hard. I engrossed myself in all the chores I could to change my inner life. I cleaned and served as much as I could: picking cotton or flowers for the images, grinding sandalwood to make paste for rituals and sacrificial fires, or washing the utensils. All this took hours of my life and yet I found no change in me, no peace. I can honestly say that matters within my thought-life actually got a lot worse. Yet I continued, in hope that one day these instincts would subside.

Guruji convinced me to carry on and said that the right time would come when all of the junk in my life would vanish. 'Leave that to me,' he said. I wondered why he didn't bring me even the slightest change if he could. He said he had the power and authority to do so. 'Mitesh, only those who are pure like me can make you pure.'

I understood that. 'Then why don't you?' I said one afternoon while I was preparing his bed.

'It's not for you to ask that question. Be patient and trust me.'

So I trusted. I'm not sure how I managed to trust him even though there was no change in my thought-life.

Chapter 9
Study and fun

Thankfully, my studies went well. I did very well in exams and so the teachers were happy. It was expected that I was to take on a very big role at some stage in my life, so academic studies were imperative. I crammed a lot of scripture, however hard it was, and developed my English-speaking skills to newer heights. However, when I read the Hindu texts, time and again I felt as if I was staring at a book with complex verses written on it. None of it refreshed me or spoke to me. There was no two-way communication or anything relational.

The Hindu faith and theology are largely based around 'doing things for God'. A pilgrimage, a fast, or a song of praise or adoration. In anything, there would never be that reply from God with a deep personal encounter. Nothing that suggested that he knew me and the details of my heart. Only one's own emotions would stir in the process. Not a drop of deep satisfaction that suggested that he loved us. For millions, it's a god (or gods) who is out there somewhere and needs to be pleased somehow so we can earn our way to heaven.

I know that there are also many strands of deep devotion or *bhakti*, intense feelings for God. Others around me might have experienced this, but I did not, at that time.

Many Hindus, and perhaps especially Gujaratis, in my experience, would rather not acquire any theological depth. 'Just tell me what to do,' they would say. Doing the right thing will enable you to overcome bad habits and thoughts and lead to salvation. Reading the scriptures can be left to the priests and scholars.

Also they will plough on with something just because they said they would, even if there are no tangible results from the god they believe in. I was the same. Like many others, I had the idea that I had said I would finish this journey and so I would continue, come what may. This false perseverance can keep anyone pushing on out of unhealthy duty and ungodly responsibility. That's what I was doing.

Along with the deep study of Hindu texts we were given advanced training in management, administration and strategy. We learned how other faiths and religions were growing by carefully studying their infrastructure. Gujaratis are very generous and tithe well and so it was critical that I, like many, was trained to steward millions of pounds within due systems and accountability, liaising closely with board members and following the organisation's central constitution. Wealth was something the organisation had no lack of.

Through the years of training the idea is that one finds his niche in the area he feels comfortable in. It could be as a head chef in a temple, looking after the images, overseeing children's activities or looking after the vast gardens in a temple. There were endless choices for what one could do as a career. I was asked by Guruji and the mentors to develop further my speaking skills in English and Gujarati, as well as administration and management. In the meantime I had to stay affiliated with all aspects of a *swami*'s life.

Once during Guruji's visit I was far away on the other side of the campus stacking large utensils. Thoughts on whether I had made the right decision for my life were swirling around in my mind again. Just then a *swami* tapped me on the shoulder and said, 'Guruji is calling you.' I dropped everything and ran. I was surprised, as I knew he had come for important international meetings. I knocked on his door and entered his room. He was waiting for me in silence so I quietly sat by his feet wondering what he had to say.

'I just wondered if you're alright. How are you getting along? Any problems?'

I broke into tears as I felt the pressure leave me. 'I can't connect with the fasting, worship, or anything, for that matter. I feel like I'm not growing.'

His kind and gentle voice went on, 'Continue anyway. Don't worry about that. Focus on me. Never forget I am the one who will take you to God. I am the one who will bring you peace.'

I looked at him and, without knowing, the words just came out. 'It feels like I'm being brainwashed.'

He sat still and said nothing. I knew I had said the wrong thing. He was calm, though, and continued. 'The guru is always right. Your thoughts should be clear that he is pure and divine.'

'Sure. I'll work on that,' I replied.

He smiled and said, 'I'm just a phone call away if you need anything. There is no turning back now. I'll help you.'

I continued in my naivety. 'Why is there so much strife and politics being played at all levels? People have been on this spiritual journey for years, and yet I see no change in their behaviour!'

His response was clear. 'It's not for you to judge or observe such things. Ignore it.'

I left the room both comforted and troubled, thankful that Guruji was listening to all my problems, yet deeply unsettled that they were not being solved and I wasn't finding the peace I was promised when I started the journey. But I kept reminding myself how Guruji was my anchor and that I'd slowly get there. When, I had no idea.

After some time, I began to miss my friends in England. I wrote many letters to Sameer and Amish but I received no reply. 'What's happening on the other side?' I asked Raj one day. He didn't respond, as he never wrote to friends. Raj was always available to give his ear, but I noticed he had a very different internal journey that I could not place a finger on. He seemed fine with the politics and corruption. It didn't seem to bother him. I can't say he was enjoying the theology, but something kept him ticking over. Maybe he was just more mature than me in accepting the way things were. He told me once not to be so demanding.

A mentor found out about my concern for my friends' lack of response from England. He called for me one afternoon in the campus garden. I sat there with him in the midst of beautiful peacocks wandering here and there, showing off their colours.

'I heard you have been writing letters?'

'Yes,' I replied, already feeling guilty.

'Mitesh, you have to forget the "other side" now. It's burned and finished. Your only friend is God and guru. Your aim is now heaven. No attachment to anybody. No affection for anybody but God and guru. You know our teachings well, so you must start embedding them deeper. Stop lending your heart everywhere.'

As he said those last few words I sensed my heart crush. I felt the doubt he had about my conviction and so I adopted a bold face and agreed. But what I thought would be a journey with friends on both sides began to unfold as something very different. It was slowly dawning on me how lonely this path was to be. As he stood to leave, he finished the conversation by saying, 'Remember, don't trust anybody. Just God and guru.'

I became more aware that in the mix of the care and the euphoria of heaven, the squeeze on my heart and mind was getting tighter.

To bring some space and fresh air from the intensity I started hosting private parties on the roof terrace. A small group of us smuggled in Western chocolates and fizzy drinks. No matter how watertight the system, I always found a way. We had a synthesiser for music and found the most secluded part of the roof terrace where no mentor would come. There were acres of space to choose from. The plan was simple. During the evening sermon, one by one we would leave over a period of 15 minutes. After sneaking away through different exits we met, ate together and sang pop songs!

In this way I tried to make matters as much fun as I could. There was an element of rebellion in this and a way to lift off the pressure.

Most of the time I got away with it. Other times, not so lucky. The dust and dirt in India can be traumatising for foreigners. I decided once to miss the corporate prayer in the temple and wash myself thoroughly with some Jo Malone body wash. It was a smart move, I thought, as all were upstairs in the temple. Little did I know that as I washed myself the fragrance would manoeuvre itself across the lobby and all around the dorm area! Very soon a teacher was standing at a distance while I was singing and washing with my eyes closed. He probably caught a few lyrics of my song, which were not from any prayer book, and then made himself noticed. I froze, hands on my soapy head and processing what to say.

'Erm. I needed a bath...' Really? Was that the best I could come out with?

He laughed and said, 'We use the local soap here in training. Nothing from overseas.'

I got the message and gave him my Jo Malone bottle. The departure was a sad affair. I clung to the local soap.

'Is this really soap?' I asked him. 'You need another bath after using this.'

He walked away, smiling. Fun was a way for me to distract myself from the core questions in my heart. It worked a fair bit, although I was fully aware that I was here in training for a reason – to achieve a deep state of peace and stability of soul just like Guruji on earth, and then move on to heaven.

Looking back, I realise that the disciplines of that time trained me in ways that I value today. But I learned them the hard way.

Raj noticed that in the mix of fun, questions and anxiety, my health was slowly getting worse. I was getting malaria nearly every six months and was constantly having viral infections. It was something I had no control over and he really sympathised.

'Be strong and don't give in to your health,' he wisely advised.

I wondered if he had similar issues. I didn't feel I could ask, as every time I brought up a sensitive subject he managed to deflect it. I realised that he didn't want to be asked uncomfortable questions. There was a very strong and decisive side to Raj that could shut you down in a scary way. Anyway, in the middle of these complex areas, my friendship with him grew and as the years passed by I began to have more frank conversations with him, which at times led to arguments. By then I knew how to stand up to him. But now he became a rock of support in my life, like Guruji. Two of my best friends in the world who I could trust and share my heart with.

Chapter 10
Fascination with Guruji grows

In 1994, Guruji took me on a world tour. This never happens. I was still in training and a lot more studies needed to be crammed in, and yet he asked for me to be in his company while he travelled to the UK, Kenya, USA, Canada, Czech Republic and Sweden. Again, I was taken aback by his love, care and promotion. I still had no idea as to why I had such a special place in his heart. The trainers in the monastery were not too happy with the disruption to my flow of studies, but they had no choice. Raj came on the team as well, which was a sweet reminder of our tour across the US years before. We took an Air India flight from Sahar airport, Mumbai. I was seated in first class with Guruji, and was excited for the tour ahead.

I arrived back in my homeland much sooner than I had ever anticipated, even though the two and a half years in the monastery did seem like an eternity. I was so glad to be breathing English air again and I realised how much I missed this wonderful land. It felt weird and yet comfortable, as in the years after my departure from the London temple community everyone, including my parents, seemed to be accustomed to my abrupt and determined decision. I met my parents, which was amicable, and we chatted about my future in a slightly awkward manner. I managed well through the discussion, and so did they.

They shared no hard feelings and so we carried on the journey. Lots had changed by this time within my old friends' circle. Some were still journeying on their spiritual path in their own casual way, with further studies or full-time work, and others were completely off the radar and had stopped coming to the temple.

The four months passed by very quickly, and Guruji kept encouraging me to speak in the congregation in every country wherever and whenever possible. This acknowledgement reinstated my close position with him within the international congregation, until my return to India and further training.

It was during this tour, however, that I really noticed Guruji's ability to raise money, and the ease with which his followers gave – close to 35 million dollars in just four months. He would quietly listen to the welfare and financial situation of his devotee and then give a figure to donate. The follower would say yes and then insist on giving more! I couldn't believe my eyes. There were times, though, when I noticed that his focus was very much on those who had a lot of wealth instead of those who were very modest in finances. He gave time to the rich, visiting their homes and sitting in their Rolls-Royces, shaping his whole schedule around them. He sacrificed his sleep and dinner times to attend to their needs.

I comprehended this uncomfortable scenario by convincing myself that he needed to please and look after these people as they were the big financiers who were funding his empire of temples. If you wanted to build large ornate temples of marble, then you needed a good handful of wealthy Gujaratis, of which there were plenty. I tried to take this all as a part of God's plan for growth and to establish the Hindu faith in the most powerful way. Yet I struggled with the idea of the poor people not being acknowledged as a result. I also realised that if you could bring in vast amounts of wealth, then the attention and recognition from Guruji would greatly increase. I wanted that place in his heart and so for now I parked the thought quite far back in my mind.

Why was my desire to have more of a place within his heart so constant, even in the midst of questions, doubts and struggles? People like Guruji have developed a very distinctive and yet attractive personality. They can speak what is in your mind as well as hypnotically give you the most powerful stare or smile that can send you head over heels. I'm not sure how he learned this, but at the time that level of magical dynamism in his eyes could only be of God, I thought. How could a simple old man, born in a village in India, dressed in orange, raise millions and millions of pounds from intellectuals across the globe, people who were managing massive businesses as well as holding very high positions in banks and corporations? It was fascinating to see the paradox of his 'job title' against the 'job level' of the people he was attracting.

There was a presence about him. I can honestly say that when I was with Guruji I felt I was in God's presence. I could sit for hours and just stare at him in devotion. I often did that, as he sat writing letters in his room. I didn't want to move. I felt comfort and security in his presence. He was my father and mother, meeting all my needs.

There's something that people like him can draw on which captivates people and gains their fullest attention. At the same time there was something fascinatingly secretive about his inner life that demanded more of your attention. At each stage he would share a very little about his thoughts and heart, which would allow you a little further into his journey until he delivered more information. Looking back, I'm sure there are many like him in the world who can convince and attract an audience of all shapes and sizes.

99

After the tour came to an end, I was ordained in England and stepped from white robes into orange. I had a new name and my title was now *swami*, which means 'one who is to be revered'. I asked if I could study another year and then move on to a place of work.

So I arrived back in India with my new clothes and new name. It felt good and the change brought a sense of direction to my life. A year passed by very quickly.

Now I was in a lifetime commitment to celibacy. No marriage – in fact, no interaction at all with women. I could not even look at a woman intentionally. If by accident I did touch a woman during travel, I had to fast. That's why we always had to travel in pairs. The theory was to encourage each other in purity and integrity. Actually, it was to keep an eye on each other. I disagreed with this idea in my heart, but it was central to the organisation for priests.

The control and monitoring around this aspect was astronomical. I learned very early the consequences of even the slightest slip. It happened straight after my ordination as a *swami*. A very traumatic incident took place which scarred me for years. I met a lady whom I knew well. I mean, I just met her, that's all. Of course, I had to make it private and secret, so a friend helped me. There was nothing illicit whatsoever in the intention. My friend was present, too. I had been close to this lady before my training and so she wanted to meet.

After this meeting I didn't think much of it. However, an explosion took place that went into orbit! People found out and Guruji was very angry. That night I was summoned to his room where I saw a very serious and different face. He sat with me and gave me the most horrific telling-off. The shame, guilt and condemnation thrown at me were heavy. That day was brutal, filled with verbal slaughter. I still wondered what the big deal was – after all, I only met her.

Other priests fell on me like a ton of bricks, as if I had just invited the devil to my birthday party. It was a chance for them to get back at me for all the special treatment I had been getting. For months I got weird looks and sarcastic comments. The general tone was, 'You are forgiven but don't forget you did that.'

For years I had conversations with Guruji that ended with this incident cropping up. He showed his hurt and disappointment which led me to guilt and shame. 'After all that I've done for you. This is how you let me down.'

I felt so sad that I had done this to him. My relationship with him had changed. It was severed. For months he ignored me and the joy he would have on seeing me was no longer there. I was stuck. Friends and other *swamis* said that he loved me and that was why he was so angry and upset. I understood them, but equally felt that love should be unconditional. It didn't matter what I had done: I shouldn't be abandoned.

Guruji had lost face because of me. He had favoured me so much, telling others that I had 'abundant good fruit' from my previous births.

'I can't help but help him,' he told others. 'I can't say no to him. There seem to be angels walking in front of him and I just see something very special in his life.'

He really believed this: it was the reason for his favour, rather than my personality or talents. Now I had failed him and he was hurt. His relationship, I realised much later, was in some ways manipulative. He could show intense love and then suddenly withdraw, putting up a wall that would keep a person in suspense, still hooked.

Guruji's anger subsided but I could tell it was still there, hidden behind a face that was trying hard to take care of me. I had access to him again but somehow he was careful about me. I wasn't really forgiven. Before, he could pick me out in a crowd of 3,000. Now he would ignore me when I was sitting right in front of him.

To please him and repair the friendship, I decided that I was really going to prove myself through hard work and bring back his favour. My affection and attachment for Guruji were still deep and he was like my mother and father, as I have said. I felt that at this stage in my life I needed correction and discipline for a place in heaven, and so I had to journey through all the difficulties of training, teaching, celibacy, fasts and ill health. I was always hopeful that things would get better, and I had my mind blinkered so that I believed it was still too early to expect big changes in me.

Frankly, at a subtle level I was now trapped. I was dependent on an organisation that knew I had a 'scar' to my name. To me it was simple but I had seen with others how the organisation could exaggerate and scar a person's character for life. I noticed as a child that whenever a *swami* left his robes and went home, to keep the congregation away from any doubt, the senior *swamis* would literally make up false, damaging reasons as to why that *swami* had left. So not only was he scarred within the circle of *swamis*, but the whole community would see him in the same light. It was easier to stay put and win the hearts of many again.

My final year passed quite traumatically because of this very simple and yet scrutinised incident. By now, at the end of 1995, I was ready to leave and be placed in a centre to begin my career.

Guruji and the mentors agreed, and so I packed my books and medication into one simple, medium-sized box. Everything I had could fit into it. I said my goodbyes to Raj. He was being placed in the capital, New Delhi. It was a sad moment. He didn't say much but I could sense a concern in his eyes. He helped with my box and bag. I said my farewell to others who were in my class over the years, and sat in the jeep that was to take me to the next stage of my life. I was asked to develop various activities for youth in Mumbai, which seemed exciting as I would now be more occupied and busy.

But in my excitement I couldn't help noticing the amount of medication I had packed. Medicine had become a part of my luggage. Training was over. But a constant struggle for good health had just begun.

Chapter 11
A sacred pilgrimage and the inner search

I decided to embark upon a sacred pilgrimage across India before I began my work in Mumbai. It would take me 2,000 miles and 14 days to cover. I wanted to see, search and pay my respects to all the ancient and respected Hindu temples of India, as well as bathe in the sacred Ganga and Yamuna rivers. It was a tradition to go on a pilgrimage before starting any type of work. To pay respects to powerful gods and sacred sites ensured that the work ahead would run smoothly. I felt I might find something, maybe some answers to my questions and doubts. I might come across something I could add to my existing view of God – a god who needed me to please him so he could like me enough to take me to heaven. I always wondered why millions upon millions of Hindus went to these sacred places. There had to be something there.

My pilgrimage began by climbing Mount Girnar, only four hours away from the training centre in Gujarat, sacred for both Hindus and Jains. I arrived in the late evening and had a nice square Gujarati meal which led me directly to bed. The next day I began my climb at 8am up 3,500ft into the clouds to pay homage to the Hindu mystic Dattattraya. I finished the climb by midday and my legs were killing me. I was sweating and in need of rest. However, it was imperative to be back down by sunset as there were lions in this vast range of mountains. I bowed to the images in the ancient temple and sat for a bit, viewing the landscape beneath me. Clouds were passing by and wrapping themselves around me as I sat. I thought of Raj for a brief moment. I was feeling the separation.

I looked at the climb I had just achieved and gave a sigh. For a moment I felt, Was that all worth it? It was a tiresome task, yet I managed to find a long stick to support my aching calf muscles to take me all the way back down. I tied my *dhoti* in a knot to avoid it getting caught in my feet and began my descent. I arrived at my place of residence by 8pm, took a bath and had a nice meal. Within minutes I fell asleep.

The next day at 5am I was on my way to Rajasthan where I would be paying homage to the Shrinathji temple in the city of Nathdwara. Rajasthan borders with Gujarat and hosts some of the most stunning palaces in the world, the most famous being the Lake Palace Hotel which was used in the James Bond movie *Octopussy*.

Shrinathji is a fourteenth-century temple that houses the infant incarnation of Krishna, the most worshipped and popular Hindu god. I arrived at my destination, took a bath and prayed for a little while. I sat wondering at the thousands of people entering the temple on a daily basis from all over the world. The varied Hindu priests were in different shades of orange with various designs upon the forehead. I looked like one of them, only much younger. I asked my fellow *swami* what time the curtains of the inner sanctuary would open so that I could prostrate and say my prayers. He was a jolly, relaxed chap from the USA and said in his chilled voice, 'Probably some ridiculous time in the morning.' It was – 5am.

'Boy!' I said. 'That means a wake-up at 3.30am!'

I did exactly that as I wanted to pray in this very special temple for my health and for my bouts of malaria to come to a halt.

The next morning as the bells began to ring and the drums began to beat, I stood there waiting for the curtains to open. I reflected on my childhood years when my mother took me to a witch doctor in London to cure my consistent blocked nose. I had a very wheezy chest and so I always needed a pump. Nose drops were a part of my dress code growing up, and I still clung to them as a *swami*. The witch doctor told my mother that I had to stop eating anything with sugar or wheat in it. I was young, and going to Pizza Hut every week in Harrow was a must. I couldn't imagine life without pizza. I didn't follow that diet.

Suddenly the curtains opened and the priest began his prayer in song. Hindu temples and their worship styles can differ quite widely, or even seem strange, but to visit the ancient ones and respect their ways is a tradition. I said my prayers to the images and asked for good health. I stood with my hands folded for a while until I was asked to move along as others wanted a space. These temples are swamped with pilgrims and so too much time cannot be taken in silence. You say your prayers and move on.

I sat in the jeep and we made our way north. It was winter and the temperature was just right. The skies were blue with a bright sun, and the temperature around ten degrees Celsius. As the car journeyed along the bumpy roads, I looked around at the landscape wondering why I had such a disconnection with the land. Somehow I couldn't engage with or immerse myself in India.

It was a long journey to the Yamuna river, right by the romantic Taj Mahal. I marvelled at the beauty and geometry of this ancient mausoleum with its fascinating history, as I wandered within its chambers. There were thousands of empty holes where jewels and diamonds once rested in dedicated love to Mumtaz.

'This Shah Jahan was quite some romantic guy, wasn't he?' I looked at Lalit, my fellow *swami*, as he was in awe of the whole edifice.

'Yep. Lots for a girl he loved.'

We were both very similar in certain ways. We loved Guruji dearly, but equally we respected aspects of life such as romance, marriage and the general value of women. I couldn't understand why we had such a strong view of celibacy at the time. But Guruji would never budge on this matter. And I had noticed that celibacy seemed to help with focus and the sharpness of mind and memory.

After our little wander, we went down to the sacred river and took a bath. According to custom, I placed a few drops of the water on my head with respect and prayed for good health and peace. The sacred river Yamuna is worshipped as a Hindu goddess, the daughter of the sun god Surya.

'How did you manage to get malaria five times in just four years?' Lalit asked.

I looked at him in a quizzical way. 'Well, I didn't ask for it!'

His question had an undertone. Falling sick often was synonymous with the desire to leave priesthood and go home. It was seen as an excuse for many to jump ship. As I bathed in the sacred water with hope I recalled Guruji giving me insight about my malaria.

'This is good practice for you, Mitesh, to rise above sickness. The body is meant to fall sick. It's designed that way. We are not the body but the soul. This way your tolerance levels will rise.'

I thought about that for quite some time before I dried myself and sat in the jeep to take the next step of the pilgrimage. What he said made sense, yet more often than not it seemed to me a cop-out from the unanswered question, as many *swamis* had some sort of sickness, one way or other. Another view was that sickness could also be a punishment for one's deeds. The experience and reality of sickness led to a theology to support it. There wasn't anything in the teaching to cure it.

Our next stop was the ancient city of Mathura, birthplace of Krishna. The streets were laden with pictures and images of this blue-coloured god. People were selling paraphernalia related to him. I had no wish to buy and I had no money. I was in awe to be in temples that dated back hundreds of years. Again I bowed in this very sacred place where Krishna was born, and prayed as much as I could. It was easy to sit and meditate here. At the time, *Mahabharata*, the epic battle between two families, and the intervention of Krishna, was my favourite read out of all the scriptures. I read its 100,000 verses four times over, including the detailed conversation between Krishna and Arjuna, his disciple, famously known as the *Bhagavad Gita*.

After one and a half days of stops and rests, we arrived at Prayagpuri, where three sacred rivers join together – Ganga, Yamuna and Saraswati, a beautiful union of rivers filled with thousands of people waiting and washing away their sins in their deep waters. It is believed that if a person takes a bath here, then he or she is redeemed from the vicious cycle of rebirth. I didn't want another birth in this earth and I knew I needed purification from thoughts of anger, so I plunged in and chanted for a while before we had something to eat.

We stayed the night in the *ashram* (similar to a monastery), and after early morning prayers made our way to the next temple. This was Ayodhya, the birthplace of the famous god Ram. This was and still is the most controversial site in all of Hinduism. This piece of land had been on the news a lot as Hindus had torn down the 500-year-old mosque that once stood here, in December 1992. The dispute was that the mosque was built upon the birthplace of Ram during the Mughal conquest, and so

Hindus wanted their land and birthplace back at any cost. The riots between Hindus and Muslims went on for months thereafter, and nearly 2,000 people were killed in the bloodshed. I had to go through vigorous security and barbed wire before I got a chance to go inside the sacred temple's inner areas that housed the god worshipped by hundreds of millions of Hindus across the globe. I couldn't stay long as security was tight. I bowed with respect and pondered over all the stories I had read about the god Ram – his bow, his marriage, his rescue of his wife Sita from Sri Lanka where the evil Ravana had held her captive. I had read the epic scripture *Ramayana* several times. I bowed once again and made my way out.

I went a certain distance to take a wider view of this fascinating piece of history, and just there in another temple nearby I saw a priest casting out a demon from a woman who was shrieking and shouting while slapping her hands on the tiled floor. I went inside to take a closer look but it was a bit too much for me. I had read about demons and ghosts in Hindu scripture but never really believed it. I saw people like that lady as having weak minds and in need of medical help. I never knew that this cerebral view of mine would change in years to come.

Our tour ended with the most interesting temple on the east coast of India. Konark was excavated by the British and dates back to the thirteenth century. It's shaped as a beautiful chariot with huge wheels and listed as a world heritage site by UNESCO. The most awkward moment occurred when I went close to see the statuettes on the wheel.

'What are those?'

Lalit laughed and asked me to look closer. I did, and beyond the wear and tear of the stone, in a circle representing each hour of the day, there were different and rather strange postures of a man and women having sex! I looked at him and said, 'I don't get it! Why are all those postures on a temple wheel? For each hour of the day?' I decided not to overthink and made my way back to the car, smiling at the same time.

It was a fascinating, intriguing and humorous pilgrimage that gave me further insight into the diversity and complexity of the Hindu faith. Which one was right? I had no idea. I was told that it was special to pray for our needs in such sacred places, and so at every spot I prayed for good health and a spiritually successful life as a *swami*. There were moments of contemplation, deep respect and reverence at the size, beauty and antiquity of some of these very significant temples. There was a quietness and stillness in some of the places, an atmosphere and a presence which I wanted to tap into more.

I did enjoy the car journey and the varied architecture, and yet I wasn't sure if I had gained anything. Were my prayers heard? If so, which god heard them? Did he know me?

Again, I began to realise that I had ticked another box to satisfy myself. Two thousand miles, nearly 20 sacred pilgrimage sites, a tired body – and still I had unanswered questions. Why do I feel so dissatisfied? Why am I so discontented? Why am I so anxious?

A yearning for a further search brewed in my heart. The outer pilgrimage was done but the inner pilgrimage had just begun.

My journey back to Mumbai was filled with thoughts of Raj. He was now placed in New Delhi. For the first time in 25 years we were separated because of our responsibilities. He was having terrible headaches and I couldn't help wondering why illness had taken root in both our lives.

I was given my task by the head *swami* within my first day and began with prayer and zeal. Immediately the numbers of youth began to grow as a result of my strategy and ideas. It was an exciting beginning where I travelled across many parts of

Mumbai to bring in the numbers through various talks. Like many things in this world, the agenda was always to bring in numbers. I remember that people were more drawn to the talks which I based on Western books I had read about personality development, and not on the usual Hindu scriptures I read daily. I didn't pay too much attention as to why the attraction to certain self-help books, as growth was taking place. It worked, so I continued. But I did realise that the belief that 'all answers' to life were within our Hindu scriptures was a fallacy. Answers were elsewhere too. Otherwise, the senior *swamis* and I would not have been reading so many books from the West, based on personality development, to gain further insight into human behaviour.

During the Christmas-time of 1996 I fell terribly ill. I was completely wiped out by a bug in my gut that lasted for days. There I was in the medical room during my favourite month of the year, pondering why my sickness was taking so much root regardless of the varied doctors I met and methods I applied.

My time in Mumbai, along with successful growth under my leadership in the youth activities, was filled with sickness. I had the flu, shivers and tremors in my body for a good ten days every month. I was consuming antibiotics like M&Ms. I soon became immune to some of them, and my gut took a hit as well. This led to a lot of stress and anxiety. The *swamis* in the temple wondered why I was falling so ill and some said openly that I was pretending. This climate of anxiety and gossip about my health led to further isolation.

I began to read more and more books besides the Hindu scriptures, to find what I was yearning for, deep in my heart. I read *The Enneagram* by Helen Palmer, who had beautifully analysed different personality types and behaviour. My behaviour wasn't changing, so I tried everything. I was doing many things for God – the list was endless – but equally not finding any peace in my heart, no stillness or rest.

At this time of searching I came across a verse in the Bible that struck me so well that I quoted it in one of my sermons. It was from the Old Testament book of Isaiah: 'Wisdom and knowledge will be the stability of thy times' (Isaiah 33:6, KJV). The wisdom mentioned here seemed to have a different tangible feel that I was unacquainted with. I felt a sudden urge to search for it. I knew the word 'wisdom' and the many definitions of it based upon my study, but this was so attractive. After my sermon, which many had applauded, a fellow *swami* came up to me and said, 'We never quote the Bible here!' I didn't agree. But I said 'OK' anyway.

Silently I read more and more books that seemed to have biblical platforms which helped me get something from my inner search. It definitely helped the audience and they were pleased with me. It supplied something to me that I could not quite place a finger on.

Guruji came to Mumbai during a time that I was ill and I sat with him in private to explain my struggle. By now I had sensations of an electric current going through my body and couldn't sleep at night. I tossed and turned. My diet was becoming more and more strict as I couldn't digest certain foods. I began to have headaches and all sorts of body pain, like sciatica. I sat by his feet in his plush and air-conditioned room and was so fed up it just came out of my mouth: 'I want to go home.'

That was it. I knew I had said the wrong thing. He frowned and his voice was raised. 'Home? Do you know you ran away from there? There is no turning back now. We are destined to burn here now in these orange robes. Take that out of your mind!'

I apologised profusely and left his audience after bowing to his feet.

I went upstairs to my office and stared at a map of the world on my wall. I looked at the UK there. 'Somebody get me out of here!' I said out loud.

The very next day, Guruji called me back to his room. As usual, all the other people left the room to give me privacy.

'I'm sending you to the UK. In orange robes! Not as a civilian. You'll be in charge of developing Europe and Russia with another *swami*. Pack all your things and get ready to travel.'

It was a simple yet stern request. I was ecstatic. I was going back to my homeland. By that time I had come to hate India. I associated it with my constant sickness. I didn't want it any more.

Before I was to leave, Guruji asked me to visit another witch doctor back in Gujarat. 'He is very good. He can read your pulse and tell you what illness you have.'

I looked up into his eyes and felt like saying, 'Why can't you just heal me?' Thankfully, I didn't. I had already said many wrong things in his presence. That would have been a tragedy.

I spent the last few days wandering the same roads Raj and I had wandered the day we landed six years before. Two years had gone fast in Mumbai, and so had four years of training. In such a short time I had travelled the world and across the whole of India. All the major temples and teachings had been exposed to me in some depth, and now I was heading back to England for the next chapter of my life. In orange.

A few *swamis* and I arrived at Mumbai airport to take the Air India flight to London Heathrow. It felt weird. I sat by the window and pondered over the previous few years. All the challenges and questions, along with fun moments. I thought of Raj, who a year later would be placed in New York. As the Boeing 747 began to taxi I thought of my parents. 'What were they thinking of me?'

We took off in the early hours of the morning and I saw the last of Indian soil. I was relieved. The sun was shining through my window and so I closed the shutter and pressed my head against my pillow. I closed my eyes and said a quiet, 'Thank you' – to whom, I didn't know. But I was glad that I was going back to London. My home.

Chapter 12
Influence and growth

I landed at London's Heathrow Airport and felt like bowing to the soil! It was a moment of euphoria. The smell had changed and that was the first relief. No more open gutters or people using any roadside to drop their waste. I wasn't sweating or stinking of dirt and dust. I felt normal again, very clean. No car horns or people pushing each other out of the way. There were queues and things were organised. I sat in the car and the drive to the temple was a treat. Everything was quiet and calm. I had forgotten how quiet the engine of a car could be. I arrived at the temple to a grand welcome of food and lots of Lucozade. I had missed Lucozade! After three years in India drinking lemon water, I had forgotten it actually existed.

After a few days of rest, we had our first meeting with the head *swami* of the temple. Each main regional temple had a *swami* who oversaw all the activities of the other *swamis* in the region. He would be the mouthpiece to India and Guruji if any reporting was required. He had his finger on all departments from Youth Development to Press and Public Relations. We spent millions of pounds on festivals and temples. It was our tradition to celebrate our many gods' birthdays lavishly. The events were always mentioned in the Hindu press so that we could attract more of the Hindu community and try to convince them that we were the only Hindu route to heaven. The public statement of lavish and numerous temples suggested that our way of worship and theology was the right way to God. Numbers and size can bring a sense of spiritual truth.

Guruji was the only person who knew how much money was being raised and transferred to build various temples. The secrecy was so that nobody would argue or debate the cost of any project he wished to do. Only he and a handful of very loyal trustees knew the global financial situation.

The head *swami* was a very kind and gentle man who was always keen to ensure I was looked after. I had to take orders from him at all times and equally I was accountable to him. The temple was a regional hub for Europe. It was run with a full-time staff of 60 and an extra volunteer force of 150. Behind the temple, the office complex housed all the departments, from accounts to immigration and visa applications. This back office supported all of our activities with extra volunteers and finances if needed, as well as maintaining the upkeep of the temple campus. It was very well run. There were monthly meetings with all department heads and board members to ensure we were all on the same page.

These meetings lasted for hours but they were crucial as this was where issues and internal strife were to be ironed out. There was always competition between departments. Each head wanted their activities to grow fast. Each *swami*, like me, wanted to be famous, and famous very fast. Also, the harder you worked, the less chance there was of people in authority taking away your position. So a constant proving of one's own worth through growth and fancy events was normal. Sometimes the meetings got very ugly and led to accusations of financial wastage as well as blunders in management. It was a chance to tear down the reputation of another department and gain some kudos for one's own. The head *swami* would try his best to iron out what he could, but there was always a limit. Some debates and grudges between *swamis* went on for years with a lot of hurtful comments and heartache.

The rules for me were simple. Wherever and whenever I went, the head *swami* would need to know. This was to ensure that I was not bending any rules regarding money or women. However, as time went by I did leave and enter the temple without his knowledge. But that was to pursue my search for something deeper and truer which as time went by gripped me more and more. Lalit was a decent and friendly companion who always accompanied me on my secret missions to explore the 'outside world' and gain insight to a greater and deeper God. Our friendship was very formal, and so throughout my years with him I never disclosed the secrets of my heart.

The head *swami* explained my new role. This was a big step up from Mumbai and a giant leap from village life in the monastery. After all that training, it was now application time into a sophisticated system that was operating on a large scale across Europe and the UK.

The global operation was like a massive multinational company. We had several thousand centres in 45 countries. International headquarters was based in India, with global hubs in major cities round the world. Each temple hub oversaw a vast region of nations and was independent to run its own affairs with *swamis* and a board of trustees. At the same time, all nations were accountable to India, where the senior *swamis* and central board resided, for major decisions and projects. More important, Guruji, who was the president as well as the spiritual head, had the final say in everything, whether it was appointing heads of temples or financial matters. He could say no to a project that had all the funds ready and yes to something that didn't have a penny. Whatever he said, the board agreed to. The vision all came from there.

This is where I had it easy. I worked very hard and smart from the beginning, but the constant backing and acknowledgement of Guruji made matters very easy for me. Wherever I struggled to change processes in the system, he would intervene for me and things would change. I had upset him a few times, but I knew he was still beside me all the way. Lalit accompanied me in all my travels and had a say in the vision. He was very relaxed and calm, and was very good at taking things lightly and not being overwhelmed.

Initially, I travelled across the whole of the UK, to all the centres outside London, as well as to the rest of Europe. This was my land of opportunity and I was going to make the most of it, prove myself and grow the numbers.

The objective was to build congregations across various cities and then buy buildings to convert into temples. Traditional temples built with marble were not the objective, as they have to be occupied by a group of *swamis* in order to look after the images. That would mean staff and money to maintain the temple as well as look after the *swamis*.

The ritual to infuse the images with spirits in a marble temple was always carried out by Guruji. That temple would then become a regional hub. It would be open all day, every day. The images would have to be bathed, fed and put to sleep, with different garments, throughout the day. These images are not like the ones in a house shrine, which can be left as they are if one has to leave town. The traditional temple is actually the throne room of the deities, who reign there over their subjects. People come to view them and to experience the presence of God, to ask for their needs in prayer and to receive answers. Once a year, the images would be taken in chariots around the temple – their 'territory'. So the temple needs two full-time *swamis* dedicated only to caring for the images throughout the day, as a mother would care for a newborn baby. The images have breakfast offered to them, then their garments are changed for the daytime, filled with jewellery. They are then offered a lavish lunch with accompanying songs, and the *swamis* will put them to sleep by covering them with a plain silk cloth. It's a form of worship that believes that the gods are alive and need attention. Dinner and night-time sleep are also in the daily schedule, as well as five corporate worship songs where the *swamis* in the sanctuary wave the lamp.

In my case, the smaller temples that I was to convert from modest buildings or warehouses were different and very simple. The images here did not have the detailed grand ceremonies that a traditional marble temple would have. These converted buildings could be closed all week and opened only on a Sunday. They didn't need *swamis* to maintain the images. The local congregation could take care of it all and still go about their weekly affairs. This cost less money and was easy to manage.

In my new role, I travelled 70,000 miles every year on average. I was up at 6am and worked till midnight, seven days a week. This busy life enabled that strange and honest voice to stay quiet in my first few years, as I focused on work.

Growth and potential were all that occupied me, and that's what was happening. The whole of Europe had only 25 members in three cities when I first started. They were not financially stable and so buying a property in any city to convert into a temple was not going to happen soon. I decided to invest in the people and visit their homes. I sat for hours listening to their problems and giving them guidance late into the night – which businesses to buy or which home to live in, helping in divorce settlements and equally setting people up for marriage. As time went by, I realised that I was my congregation's 'go to' place for everything. It was all a part of being a *swami* and they loved me for it and showed it in various ways.

Very quickly I gained the trust of the board and the people I was overseeing. Things grew very fast with smarter operating systems and new leaders. I was able to use volunteers effectively, as members from the London temple began offering to help in increasing numbers. I gave them training and they visited the new centres in 15 or more European cities, from Lisbon to Moscow. The congregations grew to more than 500. I was now beginning to feel worthy, with a purpose. I was climbing the ladder of a successful *swami* very fast. Internationally, people saw the rapid growth in Europe and began to acknowledge my achievements.

The whole global operation was smoothly connected to governments, from Downing Street to the White House. Cash flow was abundant as the donations were regular and generous, so governments knew we meant business. Connections with governments in Europe were important for me in order to establish temples without opposition. So I began to meet British and Indian ambassadors across Europe and Russia. I sat with them to inform them who we were and what we wanted. They would then advise me how to work with the government with an understanding of the political climate.

This was necessary. Not every country comfortably allowed Hindu temples to be established, for a variety of reasons. I learned this from a bitter experience in Paris. The trustees in London were a group of down-to-earth successful businessmen. If I could raise the funds for any centre in Europe, they would give the initial stimulus and get the temple project moving. But my proposals had to be precise. My presentation for Paris was a piece of art. The figures made sense and the board very quickly shifted a large sum of money into a European account. But to my shock, a year into the project, the French government changed in the general election and so did their views on Hindu temples. They had had a very bad experience with a certain Hindu sect which was brainwashing their children and stopping them from integrating with society. This led the government to ban Hindu faiths. Our project was stuck. Hundreds of thousands of euros were now sitting in a dead temple property that was not allowed to be used.

The chairman in his kind voice called me to the board meeting. '*Swami*, next time do your homework! Not just finance, but political as well.'

I left the boardroom feeling I had just been punched in the stomach.

I realised the importance of the political climate. So my conversations with diplomats and local politicians took on a further intentional dynamic. I really had to spin to them, with backing from the local Indian ambassadors, that we were safe and legitimate. We had a good track record with our finances and adhered to government charity taxes, and we were well respected throughout the world. It was tough, as they were not so easily convinced.

More PR and shine with a touch of diplomacy was what I needed to establish myself with our temples. We needed planning permission in all these nations to have an official Hindu presence. Our good relations with the government in London helped us in other parts of the world. They were rightfully convinced that we were building community very well, and that we Gujaratis were contributing well to the economy. We had pamphlets with photographs of various world leaders who visited us. We told governments about our good work: the way we built community, how we helped Gujaratis find jobs, how our temples being present in certain cities had helped the crime rate go down. Drug dealers and muggings declined wherever we managed to set up camp.

Once, while our delegation was waiting to meet the Portuguese president, a very wealthy Indian who had orchestrated the meeting told me, '*Swami*, if you want to get to where you want to be, you'll need a web of connections.' He made sense. This idea of getting very 'connected' pushed my thought patterns towards a more business-type spirituality. I was feeling very successful, and a sense of achievement had risen in my heart as I was applauded by Guruji and all the board members for the recognition we were getting across Europe from diplomats and certain politicians. On several occasions I preached to Hindus working in the UN, chemical weapons inspectors and other international civil servants.

This association with the higher echelons of society was now my social climate, and it felt really good. My soul had darkened further for more recognition.

Chapter 13
Afraid to choose

While my project in France was still on hold I came down with a serious gut infection. A famous Harley Street surgeon, Dr Chatterji, looked into my situation. I was in bed for ten days in a secluded room and the stillness was not fun. The voice came back. It was strong, and again very honest. I was lying in my bed pondering all my prayers and pilgrimages, the blessings and encouragement from Guruji – and yet I was back in hospital. However, I noticed myself quietly enjoying my personal space and time away from the temple, its rituals and activities. I was chatting to normal people from different backgrounds. I spoke to Dr Chatterji, who had become a good friend. He was aware of my inner struggle from our very first meeting.

'I like it here,' I said.

'You like it in hospital?'

'Yes.'

'Well, it's not a good home, you know.'

I knew that and something blurted out of my heart: 'It's better than my home!'

He looked at me with the deepest concern and said in a quiet voice, '*Swami*, I think it's time you changed your home.'

Where would I go? Who would give me a job now? How could I start a normal civilian life at this age with no bank account or savings? No home – would even my parents take me back? However uncomfortable I was, at least I had a career where people respected me, and a roof over my head. With no options for manoeuvre I had to battle against the truth.

He left my room and I lay back and stared out of the window. Just then, the silent voice spoke: 'He is right. A change of home is what you need.'

It had surfaced again. That unfulfilled search for a deeper purpose in my life was back. I knew I was deeply dissatisfied with my connection with God. It wasn't what I had hoped for. I could not feel the God who had made this beautiful universe; neither did I know if He could hear the pangs of my heart. I wasn't changing, regardless of what I was doing for Him, and I just kept doing more, through Guruji, with the hope that things would change. They weren't, and, in fact, the desperation was getting worse.

At that very moment Raj phoned from the US and asked how I was doing. He was now well established and overseeing a lot of work. I began to share my thoughts and questions. He calmed me down. 'Mits, we are in this now. Let's just finish it to the end.' I wasn't happy with that answer. I put the phone down and wondered why my brother never paid heed to my clear and sensible questions.

Just then my friend Pratap walked in with my favourite Paatchi chocolate. Pratap was one of my close friends who always found time to be with me and cheer me up. He was a good listener, with a big heart and generous in many ways. He smiled and said, 'You're the only *swami* in the whole organisation who gets such high-profile treatment.'

'Yes. I know and I'm thankful,' I said. 'But do you think that's an achievement?'

He smiled. 'This place is full of celebrity and world leaders.'

I stared at my dear friend. 'Are they all as empty in heart as me?'

I left the hospital feeling shaken as I had had time to think and listen. My PA was ready with his emails and questions – a whole list of decisions I had to make. Anil was the best: brilliant at drawing charts for forecasts, and incredible attention to detail. He didn't miss a thing and was very loyal. I knew his gifts and skills and had wanted him on my team. I had done the typical Patel thing. 'You want to work for me? For free? I don't have any money to give you.'

He had laughed and surprisingly agreed. I had asked him to check with his wife and daughter first. He had had a very good job in a petroleum company and so this meant a change in lifestyle.

His family agreed and from that day my operation for Europe and Russia became smoother. Together we developed a team of ten to whom I began to delegate a lot of my work and decisions. Conferences, venues and agendas were set by them and they were very smart, loyal and trustworthy. Funds and accounts were looked at in detail, and I was given precise reports on a monthly basis. My skill at developing people and teams made me free again.

I felt that worked against me: the voice would be back in such moments. So I researched into the idea of a property in the West End. I saw what other wealthy organisations and religions were doing there. There would be a huge demand for a social centre with a library, café and lounge area for those studying and working in Central London, if it was presented well. It was a way to bring people together midweek, a trendy spiritual lounge for meditation and casual chat in a beautiful area of the West End. Many years ago, a top PR firm had told us that location is key: 'Your address matters, *swami*.'

I had the most incredible fellow, Manish, handling my PR side, and he found a property that was a good size and price, before it came on the market for the general public. The board were happy to come and view the property. Immediately my chairman liked it. He turned to the owner and said, 'We can give you £2.3 million in cash within a week.' My eyebrows went an inch higher as I realised it could happen! The owner replied that it was on auction and would go to the highest bidder. The chairman smiled, and within a day, somehow we knew all the bids. We put in an extra £50,000 and got what we wanted. Or, what *I* wanted.

This was my next thing to stay busy. Europe was on autopilot and I suddenly had the chance to develop a whole new concept. A postcode with a West End address was key for PR and spin. This was an area where my thoughts were now beginning to align. I had friends who had links with big PR firms and I began to read and think over the whole idea of spin from various people in the political world. It gripped me hard and very soon I was in bed with spin, marketing and campaigning my own work and ideas with smart, smooth and sophisticated words. It was another method to prove myself and my worth. Very quickly, Guruji noticed the speed of my success and gave me the backing I needed. He saw the vision I had, to bring a presence to key cities such as Geneva, Moscow and London's West End.

My journeys and travels continued. I was loved and revered by thousands across the world, owing to our successful growth and the charm in my talks. I had earned the love deservedly, I thought. Wherever I went, photographs would be taken and recordings of my talks began to fly across the planet. I allowed myself to be blinded further by this attention. The people I oversaw were in awe of me, catering for my every need. I didn't even have to ask. Before I could realise the cold in my feet, a mat

would be there! My shoes brought to me, my car door opened…
I just had to ask and it was there. Water? Ice cream? A new pair
of shoes? A walk along the beach? I did love the people and they
loved me too.

The Hindu followers across Europe had varied businesses,
from restaurants to clothing or professional jobs in banks and
international corporations. Whatever their work, I noticed that
Gujarati Hindus were very loving, kind and gentle. They
submitted to orange robes very quickly and preferred not to
think or question things like theology or whether they were on
the right path.

Once I was sitting by a beautiful lake in Norway when I
turned to a few who had gathered there with me. 'Don't you ever
wonder whether I'm teaching you the truth?'

They replied unanimously, '*Swami*, look at your sacrifice.
You've given up your parents, the desire for marriage and
money. If you're not telling the truth, why would you take such
a step in your life?'

Hearing them, I felt that I did have a desire for marriage, and
I missed my parents, but I said nothing. This wonderful
community of people were prepared to do anything I said, just
as I was for Guruji.

They had a need, I knew. What it was I didn't know, but I
was supplying something for them. I was in need, too, and yet I
hid it from them well. I continued to pretend that all was fine
and smooth and that kept them smiling. The dynamics of Hindu
culture are similar at all levels. Those who are respected and
honoured within a family or a faith will always have to show a
bold face. If ever they show some vulnerability or weakness to
the people below them in the system – the family or, in my case,
the congregation – the foundations of their belief would
crumble.

Close, inner friends noticed my gifts and talent and kindly challenged me now and then. Akash looked after all my travel. '*Swami*, you know with your gift of communication you could do very well if you were in the world?'

I gave the standard reply I had been taught: 'They're not my gifts but the gifts given to me by the organisation through training.'

He was frank. '*Swami*, I know you too well. You've had many of your gifts since childhood and they are yours only. Sorry if that rattles your cage, but it's true.'

'Akash,' I said slowly, 'my cage was rattling in my first year of training. Now it's do or die.'

He pressed on, 'You don't have to die. Just move on!'

I laughed and said, 'What will I do after all these years of being in this system? Look what happens to all the *swamis* who leave. They have a very tough life!'

He couldn't say more as he knew I was too late in the game now.

We walked back and went up Primrose Hill where I admired the city I loved the most. Just then my schoolteachers came to mind. I wondered what they had expected my life to turn into. Would they be happy to see the Mitesh they once knew in this struggling inner condition? Fear had kept me here and it was fear that was driving me on, fear of the unknown. I may have known so much about life through my travel and the hundreds of people I met, but I still didn't know what it was like to live the life they were living: the hardships, the challenges, the raising of children. All my friends were married and living in beautiful homes with children. My comparison was my fancy life with many homes that were not mine, along with the hundreds who followed me. Just then I knew I'd love to be in the position of being married and having kids in a comfortable home. But I was now edging on 30 years old and I knew that the world would never offer me a job or career that would financially support my desires to be a simple family man. Nobody would look at my *swami* career and give it any value in a worldly context. It's not something you can put down on a CV and apply for a job.

I was also repeatedly hearing from friends how hard they were finding certain aspects of life, like marriage and mortgages. I viewed life through the narrow lens of a very small Gujarati community, and concluded with a saddened heart that marriage and working in the world must be a nightmare. I wasn't totally convinced, and I still dreamed of it, but fear of taking that risk made me stay put.

I remember once I phoned Guruji about a friend who was going through a divorce. Guruji took the details of the case over the phone and then said, 'See! This is what I've saved you from!' His way of convincing me was that if I were in the world I'd be in the same situation.

Akash challenged me that day, however, and I couldn't shake it off. His life was much broader than many typical Gujarati family men. He wasn't regular at the temple and hardly ever sat in sermons. Yet his character and personality were admirable. He was the only Gujarati I knew who had a dog – and he loved his dog. This idea was ridiculed by many *swamis* and others, but I saw his affection for his dog, Sami, and thought that there was something special there. Once Sami fell ill and Akash phoned me at 11.30 at night. I thought the worst had happened, but it was a prayer request for his dog. I loved Akash, but somehow could not connect with this relationship with his dog. I prayed with him for his dog over the phone, and put the phone down in confusion.

I'm missing something here, I thought. There was something very beautiful in his love for his dog that I didn't know about. It struck a chord in my heart that I never knew existed. I never knew that one could love a dog so much. I was supposed to be thinking only of Guruji.

As usual, after a lot of thought, I switched my brain off and made a call to my PA to catch up with work. My phone was a good tool to keep me distracted from my deepest search of something true. I used it well.

Chapter 14
Questions

My fame was growing. I had visited Europe many times, and everything was operating with precision. I saw how my influence was moving beyond temple borders. My trips to the USA were regular, and it made me proud to know that the attendance at conferences would increase sharply if people knew I was coming. They loved the flow of my words and my way of bringing new ideas from other sources to illustrate the Hindu scriptures that I was preaching on. I told stories from my experiences, and introduced concepts from my wider reading. Later on, after President Obama was elected, I took to listening to his speeches. I liked the way he used words and constructed sentences. It was an insight for me to learn for my talks and refine them further.

During an earlier successful visit to the US, I was forced to reflect yet again on the purpose of my life. I had spoken to Raj before I left, as I was still having problems breathing through my nose. It stayed blocked most of the time and I was too busy to attend to it.

'America's best ENT surgeon is in New York, Mits. He is a friend of mine. Let's get your bloods done tomorrow morning, and then I'll send a driver to take you into Manhattan to see Dr Rajesh.'

I woke up early the next morning. It was sunny and the New York air breathed a lot of life. It was 11th September 2001. The GP arrived at my residence late for the blood tests and I was annoyed. After meeting Dr Rajesh, I had planned to go for a walk and wander around the World Trade Center, before attending a conference. The doctor took my blood and I dashed to the car.

We left swiftly for Lower Manhattan. As we were approaching Holland Tunnel, I noticed one of the twin towers on fire. 'That's weird,' I said, and my brain started buzzing. After a few more bends, to my shock I saw the second tower on fire. Suddenly the traffic in front came to a halt. The road on the other side exiting Manhattan was empty.

'What on earth is going on?' I asked. Just then, from behind, a river of ambulances, fire engines and police cars swarmed past us towards the tunnel. A policewoman shouted, 'Turn around and go back!' I switched on the radio, and the news presenter announced in shock that the first tower had collapsed. We arrived home and turned on the TV. Right before my eyes the second tower crumbled, and thousands of people with it. I couldn't look any more. I had been up those towers a few times. I had a friend in one tower who died that day. We shared the same birthday.

Suddenly the penny dropped. What if I had left early? My meeting with Dr Rajesh was a few blocks away and I would have been by the towers in time for those evil collisions! It was a lot to process in one day, but I reflected on my life a little more. God wanted me alive and made arrangements that day to ensure that. What did He have for me?

My operation with Dr Rajesh was a success. Raj decided to stay with me for a few days in Manhattan as I was still in pain. After I had had enough rest, he suggested a visit to a church in

Chicago. 'It's a megachurch,' he said. 'They have a weekly attendance of 8–10,000 people.'

I was in awe. 'What? That many Christians get together on a Sunday? What's the name of the church? Who is the leader?'

I couldn't believe my ears, as I thought churches had lost their members, and if there were any they'd be a handful in an antiquated building.

'The church's name is Willow Creek. The leader is a man named Bill Hybels.'

We flew to Chicago to visit this concept of Christianity that was new to me. The people we met were very kind and showed us around the whole complex. I felt as if I was in NASA's command centre. It was huge and so sophisticated.

One of the guides asked me, 'So, how do you receive God's love?' I was puzzled by the question and had no answer. It troubled me that I could not answer a simple question. A part of my heart suddenly leaned towards something else. Raj had exposed me to something that really pushed my boundaries. Besides the magnitude of Willow Creek church, I couldn't help but notice that the atmosphere in the whole complex was very special. There was a gentle peace everywhere that was very attractive. Normal people without robes were carrying a peace I did not know of. It seemed sad only to have had a touch of it within the hour of our visit.

After saying my goodbyes to Raj, I boarded my flight to get back into the busyness of life. A few months later, as I watched *Star Wars: Attack of the Clones*, I recalled that question in Willow Creek church. In the film, senator Padme said to Anakin Skywalker, the Jedi knight who loved her, something along the lines of, 'You're a Jedi knight and you're not allowed to love.'

It struck my heart. I realised that I was in the same position. I was not allowed to love. Maybe that's why I couldn't answer the question. I was allowed to care for people and attend to their needs, but I could never have a deep affection for anyone. All my affection had to be diverted to Guruji, and that seemed to be getting harder.

The years went by. 2007 and 2008 were years of fear and failure for many. The whole financial calamity and seeing a few dear friends lose millions brought another fear into my heart. The world seemed too unpredictable to live in. 'What would I have done if this had hit me and I had a family and a mortgage?'

I used another mental technique to suggest to myself that I was better off. I had no mortgage. I was still eating well and travelling as usual. My medical check-ups were still in the same private hospitals. I began to latch on to horrible situations of people in the world, or of those close to me, and by comparison made myself feel better.

At the end of 2009 I went to India for a meeting with Guruji and the CEO of the whole organisation. I had never liked India, so I planned to stay only five days. The CEO called me to his office. He was an elderly *swami* who had the most incredible mind and the patience of a bear in a chilled swimming pool. I sat and wondered what was up. Good news? Bad news? As his words flowed, they were music to my ears.

'We need you to travel and preach more of the ancient Hindu scriptures that we have built our foundations on. There are not many brilliant speakers like you. Europe is something I would like you to delegate more. Keep up the work in the West End. But now I want you to come to India and sit with our scholars who have been studying for 20-odd years. Learn from them the deeper meanings of our theology and then translate it into English. The West needs more depth, and you have to supply it. You have free access to come and go when you wish. I want you to travel to the US as well and preach there, in every major temple and centre.'

I left his office elated, excited and overjoyed with this next, even higher profile job in my *swami* career. I had been chosen to do the most demanding thing yet in the history of the organisation, and I wasn't going to let anyone down. I already had teams in Europe and the West End managing work according to my vision and advice. I was now extending my influence beyond these borders. I thought of the whole world and the endless countries I would be visiting. A new beginning.

As with all things, my visits and studies in India started well. I came every few months for a few days, and it gave me a chance to sit with Guruji, too.

'This is nice,' he said. 'This way I get to see one of my favourite *swamis*.'

I was chuffed.

I sat with scholar upon scholar to listen to the deeper ideas, philosophy and theology of the organisation, and initially found it a nice intellectual challenge. I had to work hard at it mentally and I always enjoyed that. But after some sittings, my doubts began to surface. I began to disagree a lot and asked some tough questions. This provoked one of the scholars who took me to the campus temple to have a chat. 'You need to meditate on this and accept it. This is your life now!'

I couldn't be bothered for an intellectual argument, so I deceptively agreed and went to sit with the next scholar. I didn't know how I was to translate what I didn't agree with.

At this point another very senior *swami* caught my questions and sat me down. 'You're a smart guy with sharp questions. Try not to ask too many or you'll get depressed with the answers. You might not like what you discover. Guruji is just another *swami* like us. We created his special position. I'm sure you're aware of that?'

I sat there, half-understanding and yet fully knowing what he was saying. 'Thanks for the wisdom! How do I go about all of this study?'

He looked up at me as I stood to leave. 'You've got charm. Use it, and whatever you read, just give it some spin.'

Great! I thought. I left India after that trip feeling like a cross between Piers Morgan and Alistair Campbell. Suddenly, I didn't like it.

Chapter 15
Exploring other methods and teachings

My journey back to England was full of confusion and doubt. I knew that I would have to continue and plough forward with what I had been told to do. There was no choice. I could not upset the CEO. He was Guruji's key advisor, with a say in every one of Guruji's affairs. It was also rumoured that he would one day take over Guruji's role when he passed away.

I was lying down on the first-class bed in British Airways, but my mind was churning with anxiety. How and why would I want to dive deep into a theology that really wasn't taking me anywhere in the first place? Fear kept me trapped. I felt myself up against a wall, a dead end. Yet I was persisting to try to shift that wall with all the force I could muster.

After a week's rest, I took a trip to Switzerland with a handful of books. I stayed at a friend's house in Montreux by the beautiful lake just an hour outside Geneva. As I opened a book, I caught a glimpse of the beautiful French Alps, wondering how a God who had created all this beauty could be narrowed down to a marble image within a temple.

I was now staring down at the *Upanishads*, translated by the famous Irish poet, W B Yeats. The *Upanishads* are some of Hinduism's main scriptures, a compilation of questions and answers between ancient sages and their disciples. They offer a deep and wide range of philosophical ideas about life and its meaning. I flicked through page upon page, impressed by the depth. These *Upanishads* summarise the teaching of the grand *Four Vedas*, the foundational scriptures of all Hinduism. All knowledge and understanding for Hindus, regardless of denomination, are in these four. The *Upanishads* are also known as the *Vedanta*, the 'end of the *Vedas*'. They move behind the gods of nature, the rituals and sacrifices, searching for the one underlying spiritual reality. They focus on the Self, or the soul, the innermost essence of a person, and the nature of consciousness.

There was a lovely rhythm to the translation Yeats had done from the ancient Sanskrit language. I spent a week reading the ten principal *Upanishads* again and again. Some were only three pages long, such as the *Isha Upanishad* explaining various aspects of the soul, and others were approximately 17 pages. I liked the rhythm and the depth, but after a month of constant recital I felt that I was staring at a brick wall. It helped me analyse the ideas and thought patterns that we humans have, but the deeper nourishing I needed was not being met.

It was here in Switzerland, during the beginning of this study, as I stared out upon the lake and the beautiful town of Evian, famed for its water, that the most extraordinary moment occurred. I decided to stand for a while and read, as my back was hurting. Just then, as I stood with my book in my hand, that voice came back.

Instead of asking me something, it simply whispered gently into my left ear the words, 'Jesus Christ of Nazareth'. It shook me. It felt sweet like honey, good and authentic. I lost my balance for a bit and then decided to shake it off, as it was the name of somebody who was totally opposite to what I represented. I was scared that it would take me into dangerous territory. I buried it quickly and sat back down again. The voice had vanished, but never that experience.

I continued reading the *Upanishads* for a while. I wanted to see how much I could gain, as I was told that inner change from these ancient manuscripts could not be met in a short time. However, after much pondering, searching for that inner reality of the soul and the universe, I gave up. I felt as though I was just reading very intelligent ideas and my soul was gaining no rest.

My next set of books was by Shri Aurobindo (*Arvinda* in Gujarati). A reader of Aurobindo, I was told by the CEO, is a true seeker of God. His works are not easy to read in English, as Aurobindo's intellect and insight into the cosmos and soul are really detailed and full. I started with *Letters* and then continued into his famous book *Savitri*, and then the mind-crunching *Transcendent Mind*.

Shri Aurobindo was a freedom fighter for India's Independence. His father had sent him and his sister from Calcutta (Kolkata) to London in the 1880s to study. In England both brother and sister lived with a Christian couple. Aurobindo's father had told the couple that he wanted the children to learn everything that was 'English'. Aurobindo went to St Paul's School in London where he excelled in Greek and Latin, and won a scholarship to Cambridge. After a few years he was captivated with the idea of India's freedom from the British. He returned to India to write and educate the Indian public for Independence. The British tried to chase him down, but Aurobindo found sanctuary in the French territory of Pondicherry in south India.

Here he took a huge turn in his life and transitioned into a deep spiritual search. Aurobindo developed his own method of spiritual practice, called 'integral yoga'. In 1926 he founded a monastery, the Sri Aurobindo Ashram, where he spent the rest of his life. He spent the last 17 years in silence most of the time, to focus his mind while he wrote his masterpieces.

I read his works with keen interest. They portrayed intense disciplines of meditation, the power of the mind and the various levels of purity the soul can attain. Aurobindo's theory led me to monitor my breathing and make it very slow, at the same time visualising my soul to be pure and still. Repeating in my mind, 'I am the soul and not the body,' would enable a deep conviction of this truth to take root and that would help my soul break through and override my body and its fleshly emotions. After this my soul would enter a stillness without interference from my thought-life.

The majority of Hindus believe that the soul or *atman* is the very thing that needs uplifting and strengthening, and eventually will take precedence over the body for it to go to heaven. The soul, however darkened by the body's instincts, is what we truly are. The body is the shell that is used as a tool to enable that soul-cleaning process through various practices.

Guruji told me that with his blessings my breakthrough would come much sooner than Aurobindo's. Thus my work continued with deeper reading and meditation alone. I spent at least two to four hours a day, regardless of my schedule. It was hard work, and yet after months my soul was still restless.

I was on a journey of improvement. But nothing was changing in my inner life. I spoke to the CEO *swami* over the phone about my progress in reading.

'The results will come after years of practice, dear friend. Be patient.'

My answer would have been simple, but I didn't say a thing. 'Why do I have to earn God's love through such hard work? If

I'm not gaining any stillness, how will I convince a congregation?'

I took a deep sigh and ploughed on with my reading. I had approximately 150 books from different backgrounds of Hinduism to read. I would begin each with the hope that I would find something that my soul desired. There would be four, sometimes five books open at any one time on my desk.

My next set of books was teachings from Swami Vivekananda, a famous Hindu who was the first sage to take the Hindu faith to the USA in the 1890s. He challenged many Christian theologians there through his rhetoric. Vivekananda did more than anybody to spread and popularise the *Vedanta* philosophy in the West. He was the disciple of Sri Ramakrishna, a respected sage from Kolkata (Calcutta). Vivekananda founded the Ramakrishna Mission, which had immense influence all across India and helped to revive Hinduism there. Vivekananda's teachings were intense and he had written volumes upon volumes. He was a celibate, like me, and had a lot of teaching on how celibacy helped the mind to stay pure and focused. His astounding memory, eloquence and teaching were attributed to his vows of celibacy.

The books took a lot of time to digest and so I took some of them to our annual European conference in Portugal. All the leaders of my operation were present for a five-day conference on how to establish our footing deeper within government recognition. My heart wasn't really present so I took to reading and sitting by the sea during certain meetings. Anil held the fort well in my absence.

After the five-day conference we all travelled to Cabo da Roca, which is the westernmost landmass in Europe, the closest to America. The view from the top of the cliff of the deep blue Atlantic Ocean took my breath away each time I visited there.

At the very edge stood a beautiful old stone Christian cross facing America.

I decided to sit with Vivekananda's book by the cross, hoping to be alone. As I read, my mind went around in circles of intellectual gymnastics. I loved sitting by the cross. In its shadow I felt comfortable and protected.

Anil walked over to me and sat down. '*Swami*, would you not like to join us over there?'

'Thanks, Anil,' I said. 'But I like sitting here.'

Anil wasn't a 'yes man' when it came to work and I liked it when he challenged me. He knew that I was attracted by the cross but he never dared to mention it. He quietly walked away, concerned and slightly disappointed.

I couldn't explain at the time the secret love developing in my heart for something I didn't know much of. All I knew was that something or Someone was dragging my attention through different ways. Whilst travelling, my eyes would somehow always find the Christian cross upon a church building or monument. When my flight came into land at Lisbon airport, my eyes would catch the statue of Christ standing high above the city with His arms wide open. I once went inside that beautiful statue. At the very top, the small bookshop had a plaque with a question to Jesus that I never forgot:

> 'Jesus, how much do you love us?'
> Then Jesus stretched his arms out wide and said, 'This much.'

I was captivated by this god who was ready to die for all mankind. His love was displayed in the most beautiful and yet brutal way. My heart was now obviously divided between two worlds. One was so attractive, and yet the one I was in opposed it.

Chapter 16
Search and struggle

I journeyed further across the Hindu spectrum and kept changing or refining my style of meditation – over sensible periods of time to ensure that I wasn't rushing to the 'next thing' but waiting for something to change in my soul. Each style of meditation was practised vigorously and earnestly in the privacy of my office or room, wherever I was.

I had my own room and so I took the opportunity to give up on my own personal prayer. No one knew, as I kept it a secret. For nearly 30 years I had used a personal prayer kit in the morning with photos of Guruji and the other gods in it. Now it was time to give up and change the method. I parked the prayer kit in my bag so that people could see I had it during travel, but from then on I never used it again. It was buried forever. Ironically, at this stage of deep study and my search to find God, I put aside this most important part of my prayer life. It was shocking but equally easy as I no longer valued it. This decision was my most powerful gesture to signal that God was not in this organisation. Guruji was somebody I loved dearly, but now my doubts about him being the face and mouth of God were evident.

As my mind was being exposed to other Hindu teachings across the whole canvas, I realised that Guruji was 'just another guru' like the rest. Each had an equal and very loyal following who believed with passion that they had found the 'right' god in their leader. I continued to listen to Guruji's talks during travel time, but I began to notice how his messages deflected key questions that I had about God. 'Does he know me? Does he talk to me? Can I talk to Him? Is there a daily walk in a relationship with a God who loves me as I am?'

Hindu teachings such as Guruji's did take me on a dance around these key fundamental questions, but never really brought me to a direct connection with God's heart. Not knowing that there could be another completely different road, I kept on trying. I knew I had an attraction to Christ, but I would never dare to take that step. It would be too drastic. I would lose everything I had and everybody I knew. I realised that the deepest desire in my inner being was to be loved by God and that Guruji, like other teachers of his type, was only touching the surface. They were not feeding the very deep needs my soul was thirsty for.

The Hindu religions have plenty of worship songs that one could sing to exhibit one's love for God. In my denomination there were thousands upon thousands. Just one of our poets dating back 200 years had written 26,000 songs filled with the love he had for our main god. The story of Radha and Krishna and their deep soul love was one that we knew well. I knew by heart and sang many songs that portrayed how much I loved God and the images within the temple. These songs detailed the beauty of the images very well, and I saw in my life as a *swami* the devotion with which they were written.

But my experience was that I received none of that love in return. God didn't say anything back. He said nothing. I sang because I was meant to, but a two-way relationship was what I wanted. I felt that my god just wanted to hear endless songs and not give anything back. All I wanted was his love: an acceptance as I was, without works, a deep love that would nourish me. I never found it, although it felt good that I did something for him.

I continued with each technique and method with the fear that I had no choice. Each method of meditation initially gave me a sense of purpose that something was changing and that I was on the verge of a breakthrough, but then the passion to pursue it would fizzle out. I noticed that my joy was not coming from God but from the fact that I had started a new method and the 'new change' was what brought me some hope, not a connection with God.

I studied the *Bhagavad Gita* again. The *Bhagavad Gita* is recognised as the essence of the *Vedas* and *Upanishads* – the conversation between the most revered god, Krishna, and his disciple, Arjuna. Krishna says here that he is everything and that all roads lead to him. This always confused me as Guruji would say that the god he knew and wanted me to know was higher than Krishna and all the others.

In the *Gita*, similar to the philosophy that Guruji was leaning on, Krishna highlights a path to peace through balancing the 'three *gunas*'. The three *gunas* are the three states of mind commonly known across all Hindu philosophies. The mind fluctuates throughout the day into all three.

Satva guna is a state of peace and tranquillity. *Raja guna* is a state of lust and greed, and *Tama guna* is a state of anger. The trick is to train the mind to stay only in *Satva guna*, which is peace and silence. It's not easy, the scriptures say, as owing to past *karma* (the deeds of past lives) certain sexual urges and anger moments interfere in the midst of intense meditational practice. This made sense. But then, it seemed that no matter how hard I tried, if ever I slipped into *Tama* or *Raja guna* during the day, then I would just attribute it to my past life. This felt unfair, a cop-out theory. Guruji kept telling me to focus on him and think about

145

him as he was above the three *gunas*, and so I did try a relentless pursuit to acquire a balanced mind, but still I found myself hitting a blank wall. I wasn't changing. My soul was endlessly restless. The noise in my mind wouldn't shut down. Thoughts were racing and racing and I had no peace.

I began to make a list of famous people who were not Hindus but had very good teachings on how to calm the soul. I bought their books with the excuse to 'study' their methods, in order to teach a wider congregation of Hindus and non-Hindus too. The objective was to offer comparative studies between all the Hindu faiths and eventually explain how our faith in Guruji was the only way to God. I had to be careful that others never doubted that I was actually trying these methods to still my soul for my own self.

Once I heard a famous Hindu leader speaking to 10,000 people at Wembley Arena. He was very articulate and managed to capture his audience. But the content of what he shared truly shocked me.

'I could have said that from a simple self-help book. Those are phrases and ideas from famous self-help books!' I said to Lalit as we drove away. That night in the arena, the crowd had gone crazy with applause.

'Well, if that's what the crowd wants, that's what I'll give!'

His talk was shallow and yet people were so easily pleased. Why were these people so quickly satisfied whilst I sat there in shock, not feeing my deep thirst quenched at all? They were smart words and clever sentences with a bit of humour to tickle the mind. I could do that!

So I took the plunge again into self-help books and began to digest the ideas, thoughts and patterns. I thought that I might have missed something simple and yet powerful. This was another chapter in my inner struggle for stillness.

The Seven Habits of Highly Effective People, *The 15-Second Principle*, *Who Moved My Cheese?* and *The Power of Positive Thinking* were some of the very popular books that I began to devour along with books by Tony Buzan, Zig Ziglar and Anthony Robbins.

As I visited bookshops in London, I wandered in different sections looking for what I wanted. In one of them, my eyes fell on a children's Holy Bible. I pulled it out and began to flip the pages. The verses and pictures were very appealing. Something or another spoke back to me as I read on. I bought it along with other books and I took the Bible back into my office and hid it in the middle of my scriptures to ensure it gained no attention. The next day I flicked through a few pages and again I felt an authentic connection with what I was reading. As my heart opened up to the verses, I realised, looking at my orange priestly robes, that this exploration was too dangerous and so I quickly closed the Bible, hid it amidst my other scriptures and opened another Hindu manuscript just to balance my thoughts. But the experience of a connection with something special didn't leave me.

I continued to read book upon book and listened to countless CDs. Surprisingly, there was something here. In many self-help books I found smart tools to help me analyse and pinpoint my specific behaviour. For years, deep down, I had known my anger. I had known my pride and lust for power and recognition. I had known my frustration and frequent agitation, sitting deep down and nagging at me for years. I needed to reach deep and change them. It was easy for me to hide this paradox from the public. My inner life couldn't be seen from a stage. But I knew my issues. I knew I was sick inside.

Through these books I found some answers. I found helpful tools to train the European leadership working under me for perfection in communication and management. I found the ideas for managing change and not controlling change very helpful. I found a way to analyse my behaviour. But that was it, and no further. My deep inner thirst was not being quenched. Nothing was filling the space inside of me that was hungry for truth and love.

All the reading helped my speeches to be more diverse and entertaining, so I continued. What got my attention at this time was that some of the authors of these wonderfully written books were Christians, and strangely, our global management training seminars were rapidly becoming dependent on speakers from backgrounds rooted in these ideas. The need for an 'outsider's' insight into our management's issues spoke volumes to me as I claimed, like the others, to have found God. Surely, I should be training them and solving their problems!

The self-help books took me a certain distance, until I came to another dead end. After a while the books kept repeating the same thing again and again, and so eventually I became bored and stopped.

In the middle of all this pandemonium I tried various yoga practices. The aim of yoga in its classical sense is 'the suppression of the modifications of the mind' (Patanjali), removing moral and physical distractions, through posture and controlled breathing. As your senses come to rest you can control your mental activity into stillness, emptying yourself into perfect self-consciousness.

A world-famous yoga teacher came to our temple to teach yogic breathing exercises, and I found his approach and teaching impressive. He had solved various health issues, such as lowering cholesterol and blood pressure levels, through his breathing techniques. He was very helpful and polite and I was convinced yet again that I could be helped. Secretly I was still in the depths of sickness and depression. I was taking antidepressants and my mind was always racing and sad. I took to his teachings and started to follow them regularly. I managed a few weeks and then once again I came to a halt.

I did find some benefits immediately after the deep and fast breathing exercises. Because of the crazy amounts of oxygen I was taking into my body, my mind became very still for a few minutes. But then, immediately, fear and anxiety crept back into their usual place and I lost the passion for yoga and breathing. Another box was ticked off my list and I was back to where I started.

This pattern of doing the 'next thing' continued. There was no other option, I thought. God had to be somewhere. He had to know my heart, my questions and struggles. He couldn't be Somebody just sitting on a throne in heaven looking at what I was doing for Him, as if for homework.

In the midst of this pursuit for a real God, my health added another issue to my list. It was my gall bladder. I took various tests in the world-famous Harley Street Clinic, and after a week or so the doctor said that I was fine. I asked him why I had a pain so strong and throbbing in my chest. He had no idea.

The pressure was mounting regarding my health. I had so many physical problems and the stress was increasing. I had to find more ways to suppress this deep inner pain that seemed to manifest in my physical body. How? I had no idea.

Chapter 17
The beginning of a secret affair

The year 2010 started with incredible sciatica issues again. I was in pain and couldn't sit down for too long. This was a problem, as sitting whilst reading, writing or preaching was a main part of my day. Another issue in my body was added to my ongoing list.

I diverted my mind deeper into my talents and gifts. I was an international speaker, and the recognition I was attaining helped me suppress my fear for short periods. To distract myself further, I positioned myself for more recognition and indulged myself with expensive and lavish things. Buying new and more luxurious items kept me busy as well.

The organisation had some very wealthy followers. All the members loved and catered for us *swamis* very well. It was their heart to see us looked after. I had some very close friends who bought whatever I needed or wanted. They could see my struggle and the tough inner life I was living. But they felt that they could not encourage me to go back home and leave the priesthood. Instead, they helped me stay in my robes by pampering me with stylish travel and fancy objects. If a *swami* left his robes and went back into civilian life, it always shook the faith of many.

I believed that there was no other way but to continue and plough on. I never knew that a God existed who would nourish and feed my deeper needs. It was a paradox that I could stand on a stage and speak to 10,000 people with the utmost confidence and equally suppress the deeper, darker fears of my own life. I witnessed the excitement on thousands of faces as I climbed upon a stage. They would be eager to listen to me, and yet I always felt a sense of disconnection with them and with what I said. I had a huge impact on people's lives and brought a lot of change to their thinking as well as to the organisation's. But nothing in me was changing. I was decaying. Month after month the vacuum got wider, the void bigger.

My very close friend Priyam knew some of my questions and struggles. He was a successful businessman who had kept a close eye on my journey from the very beginning. Priyam helped me fill these gaps with luxuries to bring some fun and smiles into my life. His intention was genuine.

Once, he booked me on an Emirates flight from London to Mumbai just to have some comfort and fun. It was the then fairly new A380 double-decker aircraft. In first class I had my own bedroom! I had never seen such opulence: the gold finishing, the service. It was another world – an incredible aircraft and an incredible insight into what wealth could acquire. I took a shower at 40,000ft and ticked another box in my head. But then I found myself looking out of the window as usual, wondering if my questions would be answered one day.

Along with this, I was Guruji's favourite, and so wealthy followers who hardly got to meet him flocked to look after me, as they believed that serving somebody so near to Guruji's heart would be the same as serving him directly. They were very keen to serve me as a great spiritual privilege. 'You have given your life and you're his favourite and so you must have the best! If our past lives were full of good deeds, that's how we get to serve you, *swami*!'

Pride kept me latched on to all the fanfare, however senseless it was. But when the roller coaster ride with its adrenaline rush was over, a gap would allow that voice to return: 'And now what?'

That voice shook me every time. At times it was quiet and audible; at other times it was a feeling coming deep from my stomach. I couldn't take the advice from the voice as my fear said no and it was against everything I was hanging on to.

I continued to run away from this voice, as I had no answer. As a *swami* it was easy for me to talk and preach about pride and yet hide it within my own life. I deluded myself by thinking of the handful of *swamis* who were just as influential and so they had the same lavish style of living. This comparison justified to me my comforts and demands. My followers would never challenge me or even dare to think that I had pride. They were all the more happy that a *swami* like me should be treated well.

Once, on an earlier visit to Geneva, my dear friend Sanjit took me to his mountain cottage. He suggested that we go into the quiet of the Alps and engage in a philosophical discussion about God. Sanjit had billions of pounds in his empire and yet he always found time for spirituality. He owned his own private bank and would always donate a few chips of gold to my work. As one usually does!

The car journey was unsettling as he asked questions about life, *karma*, reincarnation and various other aspects of the Hindu way of life and the hereafter. I knew that my answers were full of deflections and there wasn't any substance in them. I wasn't convinced myself about all my readings, and so how could I convince him? He saw the lack of interest on my face. He glanced at me and in a very diplomatic way said, 'You're not a very happy *swami*, are you?'

I stumbled over my words. 'Oh, I am, I am!'

He knew I wasn't telling the truth. He continued, 'I'm bringing Michael Jackson to meet you guys next year. He's a friend of mine. Talk some sense into him, will you? He needs it.'

I looked at Mont Blanc in the distance and laughed at myself in silence. 'Talk some sense into him? With what?' Just then I thought of his song, 'Man in the Mirror'.

My awkward moments in the midst of my fancy lifestyle continued. I was at London's St Pancras station ready to take the train to Antwerp. Lalit was with me, as well as two youths. On the train, as I dozed off, a voice from across the aisle came my way. 'Excuse me. Are you the boss of this group?' I looked across at this smiling black vicar. I was too tired for a rundown on Hinduism so I asked Lalit to show him one of our fancy leaflets that showed our amazing work along with the world famous leaders we were associated with.

I was dozing on and off when the vicar took out his Bible and said, 'Can I share something with you?' I kept my eyes closed to ignore him, but in my heart I was very impressed with his passion. We were dressed in orange and were forerunners of a leading Hindu faith, but that did not deter his passion. He taught from the Bible about the God of love for 45 minutes!

Later I said to Lalit, 'Why don't I have that passion for our faith? I don't know anyone in our whole organisation who would dare to do that, and with so much love and respect.' Lalit was speechless at my thoughts. I went back to sleep with my mind thinking of this wonderful vicar who was speaking something that resonated as truth.

We arrived in the city of Antwerp, home to some of the world's most successful diamond merchants. One merchant had the most beautiful home with diamonds on all his lampshades! His home was worth millions of dollars and he personally gave me an open invitation to use it as and when I wanted.

I remember sitting beside him one evening as he shared the sadness of his heart. 'I have all these beautiful things, *swami*, but I have no peace. I have no joy.'

I sat there looking at his sad face amidst the wealth of his home and thought, You are no different to me. I feel the same. I consoled him a little and prayed for him briefly, acknowledging that I needed prayer or a miracle for my sadness too.

The more I exposed myself to the high life to ignore my issues, the more I was being reminded of them, challenged and questioned. The next day I went to visit another merchant whose home was like a museum, full of beautiful artefacts, handwoven rugs, ivory antique lamps and a driveway full of luxury cars. That night he came to our meeting and sat beside me. After a short while he turned and said, '*Swamiji*, would you pray for peace in my heart?'

I couldn't believe it. He had everything and so did I. He had wealth and I 'had God' and wealth! It was an ironic moment: a billionaire and a Hindu priest meeting together in search of peace. That would have been a photograph! Two individuals on completely separate paths, searching for peace and solitude. Yet both, after years of 'success', were dissatisfied!

I said whatever was in my heart at the time and gave him some comfort. He felt rested with my words, I could see. But I wondered who would give me the rest I needed.

As I became the mouthpiece to Guruji for many in my region, the more my tiredness and depression increased. I wasn't really fit to answer their questions as my heart was now full of doubts. The frustration led me towards my close friends who paid and accompanied me on secret holidays to cheer me up and keep me smiling. They loved me and they wanted me to be happy. I knew that holidays were not the answer to my inner quest, and yet I took the opportunities and made the most of them. Having fun was another form of distraction as a substitute for the joy I needed.

I travelled to Venice later that year, with Pratap and other friends. We were riding round the islands in a speedboat, and with Pratap's encouragement I had a quick handling of the wheel. The onlookers were very amused. They took photographs of me behind the wheel with my orange robes flying here and there in the wind.

On another occasion, we hired a big ferry for a meeting on the Bosphorus. During the meeting I went up to the top deck and said to the captain, 'I want to drive the ferry, please.' Looking at my clothes he had no idea what to say, and simply nodded. I took the helm for a while as the captain stood there, no doubt with his heart beating rapidly.

My fun was actually a way of showing how fed up I was inside. It was a facet of rebellion against some of the rules, as well as frustration at not getting what I really wanted, which was God's true and real love.

Raj was also beginning to ensure that I had some fun and downtime. He was a little worried by my questions and hoped that they would be outweighed by the luxury, comfort and absence of financial worry.

Once Raj, a few other *swamis* and I sat for a few hours in a Jacuzzi, chatting and laughing. Raj looked at me and said. 'Mits, how many people in the world do you think have the comforts we have?' I saw what he was saying: it wasn't a prideful gesture but more of a 'count your blessings' suggestion.

'Not many, Raj. I know. Many people have not seen the things or travelled the way I have, but I don't feel that's the objective of life. We did this journey together as we saw God in Guruji. It was to get to a heaven. I feel we, or at least I, have lost that passion, simply because I don't believe it any more.'

His smile dropped. 'Mits, you have been loved by Guruji like none other. We can't let him down.'

I saw the sense but then I hit the target. 'Don't you feel that he has let us down by not telling us the complete truth?'

He was annoyed at that. Raj had a loyalty that was way above my bar. 'You are going too far, Mits!'

He left the Jacuzzi and walked away and went to bed.

At one time I drove with Pratap past the Brompton Oratory in London's South Kensington.

'Pratap, let's go inside that church, shall we?'

'Sure,' he said. '*Swami*, it's the choir associated with this church that sings in all *The Lord of the Rings* films.'

I loved *The Lord of The Rings*. As we climbed the steps into this beautiful Catholic church I remembered the scene in the second film when Samwise Gamgee says to Frodo Baggins, something along these lines: 'Mr Frodo, even if there is the smallest amount of good in this world it's worth fighting for it.' Frodo had lost heart as darkness had taken over. This beautiful birth of hope from Samwise struck every chord in my heart.

As we entered the majestic church dedicated to the 'Messiah', Pratap smiled at me and said, '*Swami*, do you think you may have been a Christian in your past life?'

I chuckled, 'Don't be silly,' yet secretly hoped that I had been.

I kept a very good pretence of just 'learning from the Christians', but in my heart I was aware by now that I was having a secret love affair with another god.

The exposure through my travels at various levels had broken through the borders of a god that I thought was in a statue or guru. Amidst the fun and frolic, I could not help but notice the beauty and magnitude of God's creation. God was much bigger than the boxes I had placed Him in. Just one visit to the beautiful tulip gardens in Keukenhof in Holland challenged me that God is not captive in an image or a guru. He is much wider, more creative and beautiful.

My arguments about our theories and theology were slowly beginning to get vocal. *Swamis* or other senior congregation members couldn't say anything, as I was popular and in demand internationally. I didn't know then, but it was brewing in their minds that I was a bit too challenging. Raj tried his best to warn me and ensure that I didn't go too far. I guess it was too late, as my heart was not willing to agree with the rules I had been taught. At glacial speed, 2010 was dragging along, and so was my spiritual walk. Amidst the fun, frolic, recognition and fame, I was struggling to maintain it.

Chapter 18
A strange attraction

By August of 2010, my secret love affair with this other god had taken my travels to Rome nearly 20 times. I still couldn't put my finger upon what was attracting me, or how. I wasn't doing anything, praying in any way or even intentionally worshipping this god, but my heart was now leaning in a completely different direction.

Each time I went to Rome I walked the streets and searched out beautiful churches full of art, beauty and culture. I spent most of my time wondering and staring in awe at the beautiful buildings built for a Christ who was brutally crucified 2,000 years ago. I had seen magnificent temples all over India and in the rest of the world, but there was a beautiful presence residing over these churches, something unique and attractive. Over time, I became so acquainted with that city that I can still today guide anyone through its enchanting streets and buildings.

Other *swamis* from various parts of the world wanted to see Rome and so I started to take them, group after group. As I walked them around, I spoke with a secret pride of the 'achievements' of the church. We were not the only people on the planet able to build beautiful things, was one of my points. At one place a *swami* turned to me as I narrated the names of the apostles, 'Remember, *swami*, our god is the only true God and he resides in Guruji.' I smiled, but my heart didn't agree fully. By now I was convinced that my path to heaven was not through Guruji. The beauty and creativity of the world around me convinced me that a God I still did not know was much bigger. I felt hurt as to why these *swamis* were so narrow-minded.

St Peter's three main basilicas were the most beautiful churches I had seen in my entire life. The art and expression of beauty within them gave me a bigger idea of a very big God. At the entrance of St Peter's my eyes always rested on *La Pietà*, the astonishing sculpture by Michelangelo, created when he was only 24. It's a statue of Mary with Jesus on her lap after He was taken off the cross. When I saw that sculpture for the first time, I fell in love with it. More than anything, the face of Mary was a wonderful combination of sorrow with a beautiful acceptance. Although the body of the Messiah was broken, slain and resting on her lap, there seemed to me a secret power still present within Him. There was a beautiful presence resting over the area that connected with me deep within.

I turned to Lalit and told him that I would love a picture of *La Pietà* on the back of my office door. 'Nobody can see it there but me.'

He smiled and gave me a weird look. Lalit, by now, I could see, was having doubts about my interests. He accompanied me almost everywhere and had been in almost every church I had been in. Yet I noticed that he wasn't feeling anything that I felt. He was very open to sit and view, but never in the awe that I experienced.

'*Swami*, I like to keep my life simple. All this is too complicated for me.'

I couldn't challenge his thought-life directly, as he might tell others that I was being rebellious to the system and theology. I still kept a façade of learning and gaining head knowledge about another faith, as I didn't want to make obvious what was brewing in my heart. In fact, I still didn't know what was brewing except that I had a secret attraction to anything associated with Jesus Christ.

I was privileged to be given a special private area by the Swiss Guards in the Sistine Chapel. My place was on the right, under the painting of *The Last Judgement*. I would sit quietly and look at the paintings by Botticelli of Jesus and John the Baptist. Sitting in my orange robes, amidst the crowds going in and out, I stared from painting to painting, saying to myself quietly, 'This all makes sense. Something feels right about this...'

I knew nothing about the stories, but I felt they were true and they spoke deep within me. There was a connection each time to a core inside me that I still hadn't explored or knew existed. I couldn't resist. I just stared and stared, captivated by this person, Jesus. There was a presence here that I could not define. I couldn't give it a name, a theory or theology. For once I was secretly fine with not understanding. Each time I encountered these moments, my foundations were being shaken radically.

In the warmth and peace of the night I would walk down from my hotel room and climb the hill to the president's palace nearby. From there I could see St Peter's Dome, with the 12 apostles along with Jesus.

What is so special in this place? I thought. I knew the history of the popes and the empire had many bad moments too, but above that a powerful Presence and peace resided there. Something was touching me deep inside. Something that I didn't have, but needed.

These regular trips to Rome and other churches in London led to my having a secret circle of Christian friends. They were a fun bunch to be around, and I noticed that they never judged me.

Manish, who was overseeing my Public Relations department for the West End, introduced me to a lovely fellow by the name of Mr Higgins, the headmaster of a prominent private school in London. Very soon he became a close friend. He was studying Hindu texts, but was also an avid reader of the Bible and other Western classics. He agreed to teach me Shakespeare, as I loved his works. This was a beautiful entry for me into poetry and it stretched my heart. I started learning sonnets by heart. *Sonnet 116*, which portrayed a beautiful picture of love, was my favourite. This led to intricate insights into another world that I was unaware of. We read *Hamlet* together on Monday nights and then dived into Homer's *The Iliad* and *The Odyssey* as well.

At one point Mr Higgins realised my heart was not where my robes suggested, and so he asked me to read the Sermon on the Mount. 'You'll really love that!'

Here we were. A very English man talking with a Hindu *swami* priest in the Hindu temple's monastery about the Sermon on the Mount. I freely read according to his suggestion. It felt so beautiful. Again and again I felt connected with something profound. But in my role as a *swami* and my learning and reading of other Hindu scriptures, it was a challenge to my mind. I was a little worried, as I thought that if I continued to read it would pull me away from what I was supposed to represent.

I still represented Guruji and one of the foremost Hindu organisations in the world, so my fear kept me trapped and distant from such Bible readings. So I would read a little, enjoy it and then stop myself. This battle continued as Mr Higgins and I sat in my office in the temple's monastery and chatted for hours on end and read beautiful poetry and Bible verses. He never forced any theory or doctrine upon me, and yet I was ready to take more of what he was suggesting.

I looked forward to Monday nights and the wonderful conversations that would take place. Mr Higgins had a huge impact on my life at that time and influenced greatly my thinking and attitudes towards life, nature and the world. After our chat I would invite him downstairs to share a wonderful Gujarati meal in our temple VIP lounge.

The encounters, experiences and moments with a different God through travel, books, films and friends began to surface in my talks and presentations. I knew the faces in front of me hungered for something more. I was feeding them the little I knew of that 'more' and thus began to realise over time why thousands were captivated with me standing on a stage and preaching. I brought them a different dimension, inviting them to look at the world around them. I pointed them to a broader vision of God, beyond the 200 years of our own denomination's history. It wasn't just my eloquence or rhetoric. They were travelling miles for what they really hungered after: a loving and borderless God.

I was invited to Orlando during that summer for the organisation's national convention. Raj was so happy that I was there and he asked me to give the keynote speech. Four thousand people were present in the Rosen Plaza Hotel and they began to clap and cheer as I walked up the steps to the lectern. By now I was used to the applause and adoration. I climbed the steps in the midst of thousands as easily as I would open the fridge for a glass of milk. I summarised the eight-day convention in ten minutes. That was the task and I delivered it, as usual, not at all nervous. I read a few texts from Hindu scripture but offered my own insight, experience and exposure based on my inner journey and this connection I had found with a bigger God through my travels and friends.

The crowd rose to a standing ovation and continued clapping and cheering until I took my seat down below beside my *swami* friend Bhavesh. He was a dear friend who lived in the US, a man with whom I had had many discussions and debates. He respected and honoured my out-of-the-box thinking, but just like Lalit his fear kept him trapped within the confinement of a bordered and sealed God. He turned to me in amazement as the crowd were still clapping and said, 'Wow! I've never heard that text in that way! How did you interpret that?'

I gave a sad smile and without saying another word I went away to my suite on the top floor. I knew what the real message was – a God we didn't yet know, but needed desperately. I gave my autograph to a crowd of smiling faces before entering the elevator.

Back in my bedroom I stared out of my window overlooking the fountain below, wondering, and asking Someone for help to get out of this paradoxical situation. I wanted to break away from my fear that there was no choice but Guruji, no choice but the Hindu faith. There *were* choices and options but my fear kept pulling me back. I felt as if I was in a battle all the time. I quietly said to a God I didn't know, 'Please get me out of here.'

Chapter 19
Final days and winding down

I pushed the boundaries more and more in the minds of the people by presenting a three-hour speech entitled 'Colonial Consciousness'. I had met a fascinating professor in Belgium who for more than 30 years had studied the Indian mindset and behaviour related to colonial rule.

As I learned from him and then presented 'Colonial Consciousness' across the UK, USA and India, I realised that I was comfortable in a system because I felt the deep need to be controlled and managed, led and told what to do. I needed rules to keep me safe and secure. Anything outside that framework and life would be drastic for me and for thousands, I believed.

This groundbreaking insight led me to give talks in the West End for those who were hungry to know 'more' about God and themselves. I used an iPad and a screen to project my ideas and thoughts. Very soon Indians from outside the organisation began to attend, sometimes travelling for miles. I didn't allow them just to sit and listen as normal, but wanted them to ask me tough questions. I felt they needed to do so for their own sense of freedom and inner expansion. I didn't know then what real freedom was, but only that I didn't have it. I would always answer as best I could, and if I didn't have an answer I didn't waffle. I just said that I didn't know.

So the hunger grew and so did the numbers of this 'special' group. Some, I could see, found it difficult to listen, not because of smart words or lofty sentences, but because I began to shake the very foundations of this unhealthy need to be controlled and led. It made some people very uncomfortable and so they began to complain to the top. However, I wasn't told to stop. I saw the value in authority and leadership. I wasn't preaching from a place of anarchy, but from a place of asking tough, sincere and honest questions about control and manipulation at a very subtle level.

As I began to prepare my speeches I realised the vastness of this area. Rules and regulations from a place of fear make people feel they are doing something for God. It wasn't so clear in my thoughts at the time, but the general gist was dawning on me more and more.

Eventually, in the midst of this flow of deeper understanding, my health took another dip.

In January 2011 I felt that my body was not allowing me to go further. I decided to park the European operation as well as the West End operation and find myself the world's best clinic. I was taking too much medication and going to very expensive colon-cleansing clinics once or twice a week. My brother, Raj, in the USA helped with the research and mentioned the Mayo Clinic in Jacksonville, Florida.

With Mayo you can't be admitted just because you have lots of money. The Mayo only sees you if you are a rare case. I was rare! By the end of 2010 I was taking nearly 40 tablets a day, Allopathic, Ayurvedic and Alternative. It was a horrible place to be. I received a referral by a Harley Street doctor and my file was sent off to the USA. Guruji, as always, kindly and quickly gave me the permission. This would cost hundreds of thousands of dollars, of which I was aware and deeply thankful. I phoned him before I left for Heathrow Airport and he said in his now very dim voice, 'Keep me informed and updated on your results.' I was still grateful that he cared, but equally very upset that he was my guru, who should have healed me years ago, being the face and mouth of God that he was. How could this god allow this to happen in my life when I had served and done so much for him?

I spoke to Anil before my flight took off. 'Anil, I'm switching off for a while now. I'm not going to take any calls regarding work. I need to fix this.'

Anil was a great man and very loyal, but I couldn't share too much of my heart with him. I knew I would miss him as this was going to be a long journey. I said goodbye to Pratap and Priyam. These three were probably the closest to my heart along with Raj and Guruji, but then again, like the Jedi knight in *Star Wars*, I wasn't allowed to receive too much affection or give away love vulnerably. Guruji had told me to keep walls around my heart so that I wouldn't slip into any affection but for him.

I had taken with me my Harry Potter books. J K Rowling was an author I had followed along with all my other reading. The creativity and imagination in these novels was astounding, but for me the central theme of love throughout the seven books kept me beautifully locked. Amidst all of Harry's gifts and talents, his headmaster always reminded him that the greatest gift he had was that he could love. The enemy had no weapon against love; he would always be defeated.

The intricate weaving of the friendships with loyalty and honour impacted my heart, and the desire to know 'love' surfaced further. I was aware that many Christians were not happy with the whole Harry Potter saga, but I was looking deeply into what the author was exposing through her characters and relationships – a dynamic of friendship that I wasn't aware existed. I was always told by Guruji not to trust anyone, never to share my heart with anyone but him. Yet the theme within these books with the three main characters suggested a more real and authentic way of living.

It was January 2011 and the British Airways flight began to race down the runway. I landed at Newark airport in New Jersey to meet Raj. My brother had a huge responsibility in the US, but equally attended to all my needs. By this time I could see his love, care and concern, even though he tried his best to hide it. He was concerned about my health, but equally happy that I was with him now. This would give us some quality time together.

'Just chill, Mits! Take your time now. Don't think of London or your work. Be at rest and get this sorted.' As always, Raj gave the wisest advice.

We flew to Jacksonville, Florida. Here I would stay with the most loving and deeply understanding family for the next ten months of my life. Nitin and Savan were two brothers with beautiful families and thriving businesses. Yet they were willing to sacrifice their time and space for me to get better. It was a picture of dedication and service that was so humbling for me. They would drive me lovingly to the clinic and back, three days a week. I would be taken on long walks along the beach and stunning drives across the beautiful Florida landscape.

It was time to start winding down. Slow down. Rest and reason quietly. Think silently and reflect on my life. These ten months helped me articulate more accurately in my head what was going on in my heart.

'You're too young for all these illnesses!' Doctor Dorsher was a Godsend in this time of my life. Laughing with me and at me all the time whilst eating M&Ms and drinking lots of cola… He was and still is a dear friend. Bright and brilliant, he was chairman of his department of Pain Management. Four other department chairmen would personally oversee my case under his advice. They were the chairs of Sleep Disorder, Fibromyalgia, Pelvic Floor and Gastroenterology.

The Mayo Clinic set-up was like none other I had seen anywhere in the world. The efficiency, service and diagnosis were the personification of brilliance and excellence in every area of medicine. One by one the doctors did various checks on me. Dr Dorsher and his wonderful colleague Dr Thomson sat with me every day to ease the pain in my body that I had got so used to. I was privileged to be looked after in such a wonderful establishment.

At home, my brother Raj, Himesh, a fellow *swami* who was lovingly caring for me and documenting all the medical reports, Savan and Nitin made me laugh as much as they could. Besides the rough and tough treatment, it was the most refreshing time of my life, just being and doing nothing. On my thirty-ninth birthday, Raj arranged a special celebration, complete with a saxophone player. He knew that was one of my favourite instruments.

One afternoon, Raj walked in and sat beside me. 'Mits, I hear you enjoy visiting churches. You've been to Westminster Abbey and St Paul's Cathedral quite a few times.' There was concern in his tone.

'Yes, I have. It's just to explore how they do things, and it's something extra to learn.'

He knew my answer was a little distant from the truth. 'Just be careful, bro. I don't want you getting into trouble. I'm convinced that you know what you're doing, but others are watching and I don't think they are.'

I knew he was warning me. 'Raj! It's only a visit. I can't stay locked up all day in temple and Hindu ideas. It's frustrating me.'

Raj was calm. 'Be wise, Mits. You're very rare and this organisation is hugely benefiting from you. People admire how different you are, your thoughts, your approach. We all want to keep you. Even America would love for you to stay here. But just don't push the boundaries too much.'

I appreciated my brother's respect for me. 'Raj, I'm not doing this on purpose. It's just something that guides me and I like it.'

He smiled with a trust that was comforting. Raj was very careful how he played 'elder brother'. He was confined by the organisation, as we were not supposed to be obvious in our love for each other. Equally he cared for my future, knowing when I was swimming in uncharted waters. Along with that, he admired and respected my decisions and thoughts. This mix of dynamics didn't help him. He felt stuck in all the emotional boundaries.

By now we had a stronger friendship. Raj knew my struggles, my questions and challenges, but equally felt helpless. I could see many a time in his eyes the message, 'Mate, quit asking and just continue...'

He wasn't forceful but more passive and reluctant to pursue the real issues when he heard my cries. He knew that it would just open up a can of worms. I understood his view and why he held on to it, but I kept pestering him with more questions about what we really stood for.

Although the new medication began to help me, and the other drugs I had been taking for years were out of my system, I still had the most horrific nights. I kept seeing people in the dark in my bedroom, hiding behind doors. If I did manage to sleep for a while, a horrific voice would wake me up and my heart rate would rise rapidly. One night, the arguing voices got too much. I felt as if somebody was running a heavy current through my body and poking me with needles. I gave a short scream. Raj came into the room with three other *swamis* as well as Savan. They tried to press my body to relieve me of the pain. It was a night of terror. I've had many of those in my life, but that night really scared me.

These months in the clinic and home helped me reflect a lot on my life. I was forced to rest and do nothing most days. During this time, I realised what was making me feel better along with the treatment. It was the freedom of being somewhat 'out of the system'.

After ten months of this life, I didn't want to go back to the rhythm I knew I disliked. I sat with Doctor Dorsher, who was by now a close friend who knew my inner struggles and challenges. He was ready to discharge me, but I wasn't ready to be discharged. I wanted to stay separated. For this reason I decided on a plan. The plan was to lie to everyone that I had minor cancerous polyps in my colon. For this reason I needed to be seen by the same doctor once or twice a year. It was a far-fetched lie. But I tried it, just to stay as far away from the system as possible. I wasn't sure if Raj or anyone bought into it, but what I saw was that everyone played along with my scheme. I was thankful that they trusted me, sorry that it was a lie.

I was unaware at this stage, before leaving Jacksonville, of what I really needed to do, the step I really needed to take. That step was too drastic, too scary. There was a huge fear in me of the unknown. 'If I leave priesthood, what's on the other side?'

I said my goodbyes to the doctors. I was off almost all medication now. After ten months not all the ailments had subsided. Dr Dorsher knew what I really needed to do, but was kind enough not to rattle my cage. I spoke to Guruji before I left, saying that I would have to come back for more treatment as the polyps might grow back. He wasn't happy at all, but agreed.

I said my goodbyes to Raj. I felt fine, knowing that I'd see him again under the lie of a check-up at the Mayo in a few months. Little did I know that this goodbye with my brother, who by then had been my closest friend for nearly 40 years of my life, would be for the last time. Raj was my 'go to' place for processing throughout my life. A rock who never wavered.

As always, he came to the airport to drop me off. He held on to my hand luggage as much as he could, and then as the gate approached, we both stopped. I turned to Raj as I was about to board my flight. 'Bye, bro.'

He replied, 'Bye, and take care of yourself.'

'Sure, you too.'

We hugged, and then he grabbed my hand. He shook and squeezed it while looking me in the eye with a smile. I knew he was sad but equally trying to be brave. We never liked parting. I turned with a few tears in my eyes and walked down the jetty to board the plane.

That was my last hug from Raj. With the hope that I'd see him again, it wasn't too bad. If I had known then that it was my last meeting with him, I would have spoken into his life and told him what a great and remarkable man he was. I would have definitely taken longer with that hug.

Chapter 20
Departure

I landed in London in November 2011 with a sense of sadness and despair. I remember a deep foreboding as my car drove into the temple driveway. The head *swami* had kindly arranged for a whole new room to be designed for me in a different part of the campus. That must have cost quite a bit. I went to my room and sat there staring at the brand-new furniture, not wanting to be a part of it any longer, but equally unaware as to how that would happen. Crossing the line into another world seemed impossible.

I couldn't help but notice the quizzical looks upon some of the other *swamis'* faces. I knew they were having secret discussions and gossiping behind my back, so I just stayed in my room and met friends as they welcomed me back home. I wasn't interested by now in Europe or even the West End development. All my desire for development and progress had deflated. The days were dark and cloudy, as was my mind. I stared out of my window at the people flocking in and out of the temple. It felt as if I was in a zoo, caged again by these natural and theological spiritual boundaries.

Anil came to visit me and realised something was on my mind, but was unsure of its nature. Everything felt more and more eerie and uncertain. I knew I wanted to see Guruji in India after a month or so, just to pay my respects after being away for so long. I wanted to see him and find comfort of some sort.

I left for India on 17th December and landed in Mumbai where Guruji was residing. At this stage all I knew was that I would be here for ten days and then I would go back to London to resume my boring, unfulfilled life. Before I met him, I was informed by some close friends in Mumbai and London that there was some stirring and brewing around my speeches and spiritual proposals. An old *swami* friend in Mumbai leaked what was to be kept a secret from me. 'There's going to be a few bomb blasts. Just keep your cool and try not to argue. Agree with whatever comes your way and don't deny anything.'

I looked at him and said, 'I've been doing that all my life!'

I was annoyed with the whole idea of giving in to live a lie. Guruji needed to be told the truth about my heart and many other things. However, I kept my cool and waited to see how the attack on me would evolve. My friend informed me that there was a deep unrest at the senior level in India as well as in London. I was surprised – but then I wasn't. The head *swami* had played a very smooth month with me, not even indicating an issue. But *swamis*, I had learned from a very early age, have very interesting political skills. I knew how to play the game as well. That is how I had learned to keep my guard over the years. Some of the *swamis* could give the Indian government politicians a run for their money, and that's quite impressive!

I was being asked some very uncomfortable questions by the head of international welfare about my 'cancer polyps'. He called me to his office very soon after I arrived. 'How are you?' he said in a concerned voice. The head of welfare had a lot of authority. He would decide the future placement of each *swami*, unless Guruji intervened.

'I'm fine,' I said.

There was a pause while he stared straight into my eyes. 'Are you sure you have this issue of cancer?'

'Yes,' I said with a defiant face. I realised I was sitting with one of the most tactful, calculated and patient men I had ever known.

He pushed further and said, 'Well, I've heard some different stories from Himesh in America.'

Damn! I thought. How will I manoeuvre out of this one? My heart began to race and he sat there as calm as ever.

In Mumbai, a case of some sort was being built up around me and I felt cornered with a sense of guilt and shame. *Swamis* were not saying much when they met me. They kept it simple, short and very formal.

It was time to meet Guruji

I entered his private room with the head of welfare, the CEO *swami* and his private secretary, who whispered as I entered, 'Keep quiet and don't argue.'

As I entered, the chairman from London was on the phone and he was telling Guruji that I was being very forceful in pushing agendas to get the funds I needed from trustees. The phone was on speaker so that I could hear it all. It was intentional. I stood there, shocked and shattered. It was a blatant lie, and I felt a jolt as I saw Guruji listening quietly. Why somebody I valued would make up something like that I had no idea.

The head *swami* was sitting with the chairman in the London office, and so he came on the phone to Guruji straight after. I sat down by Guruji's feet while he continued on the phone, without acknowledging my presence. The head *swami* was firm: 'I don't want him back in my temple in London, Guruji. He's confusing the youth with his ideas about God, and people are debating whether he is right or wrong!' It was very well-orchestrated, but I had seen this done before. The senior management were geniuses when it came to manufacturing a case against anyone to get their own way.

I had sensed for a while that something was brewing, but not to this extent. I was sure that I would get my solace from Guruji, who always backed me up and helped me out of tight corners. This was his promise from the beginning. But he was silent, listening to the discussion in the room without offering me a chance to speak. I knew, this time, things would be different. He gave the phone away to his secretary, and sat there looking cross. I was touching his feet with respect and knew that he was not the person I had known for years. I knew my eyes were begging for no punishment.

'Before you came in the room, Himesh was on the phone to me from America as well.'

There was no 'Hello' or 'How are you?' He didn't ask about my health or any aspect of the last one and a half years since I had last seen him. The affection and care had vanished.

'Why don't you start the talking?' he continued. His soft voice had a touch of anger that I could sense would explode at any moment.

There was no point in reasoning, so I confessed that I had lied about my cancer and began to explain why, but he wasn't prepared to listen.

'I'm very sorry, Guruji, please forgive me.' I had my hands pressed against his feet.

'I'm not willing to listen to a sentence from you. You lied! How dare you lie?'

I was about to speak when the head of welfare said, 'Everyone is upset with the amount of time you stayed in the US!'

I was shocked. 'Well, I had five doctors overseeing my issues and it was serious!'

Just then Guruji jumped in, 'Is this how you repay me?'

I sat in silence. He continued. 'Your theology is also in question! What are you thinking and reading?'

Again, I kept silent. He kept hurling accusation upon accusation and made me feel worse. He then told me that I had to stay in India and spend time in the villages, or spend time in the most remote and least populated towns of the US. Not London.

'I don't want you going back to London! You have been influencing people there with the wrong doctrine. I have heard from the head *swami* and other sources.'

My back was against the wall, but for once I decided to fight. 'No! I'm not going anywhere in India!'

Just then the CEO *swami* intervened, saying that I should stay in India and get my theology straight and firm from the senior *swamis*. I felt that was ridiculous. I knew that I wasn't the only one debating the theology of the organisation, but I was on the hit list. So I didn't reply. Emotions were high. Everyone was discussing where I should live and how I should think, which was bizarre.

After some debate, Guruji said, 'Decide what you want to do!'

All eyes were on me. The temperature suddenly rose and my heart rate increased. There was silence and I could feel the eyes of apprehension on me, like daggers. I knew then that they had all pre-planned the way they would mount the pressure. They knew that the villages of India would do the trick to keep me quiet and away from influencing others.

Guruji spoke again. 'You've been confusing some of our followers in your talks. You need to go back to basics and really reaffirm your loyalty.'

I sat there listening to the verbal slaughter. He wasn't finished.

'Have you forgotten what I've done for you over the years? The times I stood by you? The times I let you travel with me? The times I favoured you above all the other *swamis*?'

For the first time ever, I saw a different Guruji to the one I had known – his anger and his punishing voice. I now realised that he was ready to throw aside anything – or anyone – if it didn't fit with his motive. He had been upset, no doubt, by the reports he had received about my theology. I had certainly been pushing the boundaries. He must also have felt hurt by what he saw as my ingratitude. But he had no good reason to kick me out of London.

Suddenly, it just came out of my mouth. 'I want to leave the organisation and go back to England... I don't want to be a *swami* any more.'

Chapter 21
Crossing the line

A dead silence fell in the room. As I said that, I felt a rush of peace, and a sense of relief filled my heart. It was the most strange and paradoxical feeling.

Guruji, who I thought would be shocked by my words, with our relationship going back 30 years, didn't seem stunned at all. In fact, he seemed as eager to see me go as the rest.

'Fine,' he said. 'Leave and go wherever you want to go.'

I was surprised and really hurt. He continued, 'I don't have the time any more and frankly I don't care.'

What I believed to be a strong bond of friendship and unconditional love for years suddenly meant nothing to him. It was all over, finished within seconds.

My heart and mind were in different time zones. It was a conditional contract after all. I couldn't understand and my brain froze. It would take months after this moment for me to process that sudden change of long-term friendship to 'I no longer need you'. But the relief overrode the hurt and I was happy to go; the desire to leave had been deep in my heart for years.

Guruji then asked me, 'Where can we send you, as your parents live abroad now?' That was harsh. I thought that after 20 years of service without pay he might offer a small home for me to live in. He had done that for many others who had left, and he had the money to do so. Surely for me, his favourite one, some money to start life again would be possible. But no, not a mention of it. It was obvious that he wanted me off his back with no strings attached.

It was a difficult decision to make about where I would go, because now I would no longer be in orange clothes. Now would be the real test of which friends would stand by me for who I was, not for what I represented. I had seen *swamis* leave in the past and suddenly the same congregation that worshipped them would no longer want to know or help them in any way. Who would want to host me now? Who would want to look after me until I gained a firm footing of some sort? I had to think.

Manish's name came to mind very quickly. We phoned him there and then and he immediately and kindly agreed to host me. He would keep my residence in his hotel a private affair so that nobody would try to access me. I would need a lot of time alone to process what had just happened and my entire life with this man whom I had loved, respected and worshipped.

My departure was not to be announced until I had actually left and entered into civilian clothes and was safely back in London. This would prevent any intervention from members of the congregation. There were times when Guruji had to revoke his decision about a *swami's* departure if certain wealthy followers intervened. Guruji was swayed quite a bit by what his wealthy members said. If the member had a liking towards a certain *swami* then he would try his best to intervene. I was glad that nobody knew about my departure as I had suddenly found some air to breathe and I didn't want anyone to take it away.

Now the standard process of departing from *swami* to civilian life began. A fellow *swami* called a tailor into the temple secretly to measure me for trousers and shirts. He came in the middle of the night while everyone was asleep. It felt very weird after years, but equally exciting. I tried my best to hide my joy.

Guruji called me one last time before I left the next day, and it wasn't a kind departure, not what I had expected. This was the man to whom I had been dedicated for most of my life. I had run away from home for his cause. I had compromised a life in England with family, as I was committed to his ways of thinking. It was my choice from the very beginning, I knew. But it was based on a belief that he loved me unconditionally and would take me to heaven. This final 20 minutes in his room defied my 20 years of belief about our friendship and love. Love wasn't in the equation after all. It was always an agenda to fulfil his purposes.

He sat there waiting for me. I sat by his bed and said, 'I'm leaving tonight.'

I was more hurt that he wasn't really concerned. There had been times in our journey together when he would cry on my departure to another city or country. But today that had all changed. Or had it changed for years but I hadn't seen it?

I waited for a soft and gentle answer but instead, 'That's good!' was his simple reply. It had an undertone that suggested, 'Just go!'

I said, 'I'll miss you!' to which he replied, 'Stop pretending.' I couldn't believe my ears. He continued. 'Don't talk or contact anyone.'

I knew what he meant by that. I had a huge influence on many and he didn't want that to continue. It didn't really concern me. I wanted out. But I did want to continue the friendship with him.

He was simple and stern. The final words came from his mouth: 'Never go back to the temple and never give a speech again in your life!'

I was taken aback. I was happy with the first request but couldn't quite understand the second. I was done with the stage anyway. I had had enough of limelight. I bowed to his feet one final time, stood up, turned and quietly left his room. More than

20 years of service and commitment suddenly meant nothing to him. Twenty years of my precious life wasted, for nothing. Baffled and confused, I went downstairs to my room and sat on my bed. I stared out over the Mumbai skyline, dazed as my thoughts froze.

I phoned Raj that night and told him everything. He was upset that I had lied about the cancer but equally shocked at the way Guruji had tried to punish me by keeping me hostage in the villages of India.

'Mits, don't worry. Try not to go back to all of this in your mind, and continue to look forward.'

'Will I be able to chat to you?' I said.

I knew the unbending rule that from the day I become a civilian, Raj, my best friend, would not be able to talk to me again. He replied passively with a sigh, 'Let's see. Just make your way back to England for now and unwind.'

His sigh of sadness gave me my answer. I said a quick goodbye and put the phone down. I didn't have a chance to talk to Pratap, Anil, Bhavesh or Priyam and thought that it would be unsafe to do so. I thought it best to contact them when I was safely in London. For now I had to get ready for the most significant flight in 20 years, a flight to freedom. Amidst all the commotion, confusion and chaos, I was glad.

The tradition for departure into civilian life is that two *swamis* escort you to the airport the day you finally leave the orange robes. After midnight, when the whole temple was asleep, the three of us, dressed in orange, got into a jeep with a bag of civilian clothes and made our way to a hotel. It had to be a simple one. We would be recognised in a five-star hotel. I took a shower and for the first time in 20 years dressed in normal civilian clothes. I couldn't hold back a smile as I was doing up my shirt buttons, as it felt so strange and yet easy. I didn't fumble with the buttons or the way the shirt tucked into my trousers. I had probably envisioned this day in my heart, without knowing, for years, and so it wasn't a culture shock at all.

I sat and opened my personal *puja* prayer kit that had been given to me on ordination day. I hadn't used it in a while, but tonight two *swamis* were watching me and so I put on my last performance. After completing this, I passed it over to the *swamis*, with my orange clothes. The rule was that nothing orange, including my rosary, would be able to travel with me back to England. My ordained name was taken away and very quickly all records of my existence within the organisation would be wiped off the system. All speeches, all events, all health insurance documents, everything. The ordained name that I had operated under for 20 years would be given to a newly ordained *swami*. This way the memory of my existence would be erased from the minds of people.

The life of a *swami* has similarities to a CIA agent, if you like. You exist, but then you don't exist. When you join, everything that identifies you to your past has to be physically and emotionally erased. If you leave the robes, everything about your existence during that time is erased again. Your identity is tethered to a system. The day you leave the system, years of your life no longer exist. This transfer of identity felt normal to me then as I was so aware of it happening throughout my years of being plugged into the organisation.

Before we left the hotel, one of the *swamis* said, 'We should call your dad.' I knew that was important. He hadn't known anything about my inner journey for years, or what had happened in the last two days. Again the tension rose. I was about to speak to my dad, whom I had deserted all those years ago. What will he say? I thought. They phoned him and he picked up. The *swami* explained my desire to depart and then gave the phone to me.

My dad was amazing. 'Hey, son! No issues. I loved you then and I still love you now. Settle down in London and I'll look forward to seeing you soon.'

I was overwhelmed with the love in his tone and words. A few seconds of hearing him speak to me after 20 years, and I was relieved. Dads will always be dads, I thought, regardless of what the son does.

I said a huge thank you to him and we left for the airport. I said goodbye to the two *swamis*, and for the first time in years I went through the immigration channel on my own. No accompanying *swami*, no fancy escort, no congregation members fussing over who would carry my bags, and no flashing cameras. Normal. It was as if I had crossed the demarcation line from North to South Korea. Free at last.

I felt as if a cloud had lifted off me. I felt awake after a long, dark sleep. The easy and casual chat with the stewardess on the aircraft helped me realise how normal I really was, underneath, all those years. I didn't feel locked in or caged any more.

But my transition across the line also meant that I would no longer be allowed to communicate with my brother, Raj. I was never to meet him again, or have any contact whatsoever. My heart was heavy. He and I had shared our hearts a lot over the years. All those hilarious and witty conversations, moments of laughter and intensity mixed with travel and tasty food... We had journeyed through a variety of challenges in our roles while accessing each other's worldview. The secrets we had shared were held in confidence and never abused, as we both highly valued confidentiality. That access door was now shut.

I fastened my seat belt and looked out of the window. I thought back to the day Raj had come to send me off in New York, less than two months earlier. If only I had known then what was to come... He was one of the last reasons why I had stayed in those robes. I knew my departure would hurt him.

People and *swamis* would give him a subtle but rough time. My departure would be thrown at him with a lot of shame.

I took out my phone and sent him a text. 'On the plane and ready to go.'

His reply, 'Congrats! Now just look forward.'

Those were the last and typically wise words Raj gave me. That's all he and I could offer each other. From this moment our worlds were no longer the same. He was still in the system that I had just rejected. I was out of bounds for him. After 40 years, two brothers, two close friends, equally gifted, would now walk separate roads.

Chapter 22
Out of the cage

I had a restful sleep during my flight. I woke up half way through and saw that I was in civilian clothes. A smile broke across my face as I looked around and saw that I was still on my own. 'Well done, Mits!' I whispered to myself.

I landed at London's Heathrow Airport on 27th December 2011 and my friend Manish sent the hotel concierge to collect me.

The journey to the West End was quiet and reflective. I was too tired to process how the last few days had unrolled. I had finally left. After 20 years of on-and-off decisions I had finally crossed the line. I was now in a car peacefully by myself – nobody monitoring my conversations or asking difficult questions. I had actually left the cage!

Thankfully, this car was not going to the temple. I arrived at the hotel where I had given a lot of my talks. That chapter was over and it made me so happy. I peeped into the auditorium and it already felt a world away. The cables, wires, my podium and screen were all in place without me at the centre. Strangely, it seemed as if the whole room knew that I wouldn't return. No more of that, I thought.

I met Manish and we sat together in his office. We had some tea and chatted about the previous few days. He said in his kind and generous way, 'I'll not let anyone know you are here. Rest. Take four weeks and just do nothing. Travel, go to the cinema, and open up your senses.'

It made sense but I knew that I'd need a job and money at some stage. Something to start with so that I could build my life again, however late.

He said not to rush but equally understood that I had no money to my name. No bank account, no NHS number, no national insurance number, let alone a curriculum vitae that would have any meaning outside the organisation. Only a British passport that suggested with a few lines my birth place and age. That was the only identity I had left.

Manish gave me money and I took his advice and wandered London's West End on my own for the first time in years. I remembered the days when I had been seated in a Range Rover or Aston Martin, just wanting to get out and go for a wander, alone. Here I was, wandering and eating wherever I chose and sitting wherever I wanted. I went to the cinema and ate in various rugged cafés. I enjoyed my favourite frapuccino coffee at Starbucks and daydreamed out of the window at the people passing by. I had no deadlines or meetings, and it was heaven. I sat on a train and it felt as if I was in Disneyland! 'Wow!' I muttered. 'I'm with all these people on public transport!' I was normal! It was awesome! I travelled to and fro, just for the fun of being on a train with others. I sat there with a smile so wide someone might have thought that I owned it.

I went into Harvey Nichols department store and spent as much time there as I wanted, again not time-bound or in any rush to get to the next place, no ushers with concerned faces. I was enjoying the randomness of my new world.

I continued my aimless wandering through the streets of my favourite city. My wanderings took me to Covent Garden, where the famous Royal Opera House is situated. This was where my journey to find my identity began.

I was window-gazing in front of the Fossil clothing shop when a young man came out of the store and greeted me with a smile.

'Hi, I'm Rahil!' he said with a beam.

I loved his name and it struck a deep chord in my heart.

'Hi, my name is Mitesh.'

He worked at the store and we began to chat as if we had known each other for years. I was captivated by his name. I asked what it meant. He gave me a list of meanings.

'In the Hindi language it means one who takes the beauty from the past into the future and leaves the bitterness behind. In Arabic it means to move from where you are to the next stage of your life and keep moving. There's also a meaning which states that Rahil means one who shows the way. Its female version is Rachel, which means lamb. And finally the Rah means one who has a new covenant with God and who is redeemed from the old.'

I was impressed. I understood only half of what he said, as I didn't know who Rachel was or what a new covenant with God meant. I thanked him and walked away with a smile. It was so strange, the way he just came out of the shop and began to talk to me.

'That's the name I want!' I said to myself. 'It's beautiful.'

My passport was about to expire and so in the new one I decided to introduce my new name for my new life. Within two weeks the matter was settled, and my name was now Rahil. A little while later I would learn with satisfaction how important a name is to one's identity.

After a few days, Bhavesh came to visit me and we sat for a while and discussed my whole departure and laughed a little about our secret visits to the Royal Philharmonic Orchestra at the Royal Albert Hall. Most of my other close friends were a little afraid to visit me and I thought it wise not to contact them. Pratap and Priyam were close to Guruji, and Anil still had a role with whoever was now in charge of Europe. They were too afraid of Guruji and the senior *swamis*. Any association with me and my derailed theology would 'contaminate' them and they would be pressured heavily into keeping away. Frankly, I wanted to start afresh anyway. I wasn't quite sure about any of those friendships after what Guruji had done and said on the day of my departure – and he was the closest to my heart of all of them. I looked back at all those relationships and I had lost all trust and honour. In fact, Bhavesh told me that some of those very close friends were now bickering and complaining about me to the hierarchy just to get into Guruji's good books and show that they had disassociated with me completely.

This was very upsetting and yet very normal, as I had seen it happen to other *swamis*. The conversation allowed my bitterness to rise. I had not been helped financially by Guruji and my resentment was strong. I had thoughts of suing the organisation under the guidance of one friend, but Manish was wise and prevented me from taking that path. I managed to suppress the hurt, anger and bitterness by going shopping and continuing to enjoy my freedom.

Slowly but surely, one by one, some of the people who had played a significant role in my journey came to visit me and congratulate me.

Michael was a very refined and dear friend who took me to many places around London to stretch my heart and mind. He was a poet and ignited in my heart a passion for poetry as well. He was very candid and for years he had hinted that I should take a bold step. He knew that I was different from the normal *swami* mould and that I had an inquisitive mind. He walked into the hotel lobby and saw me seated in normal civilian clothes. He recited a few lines from Shakespeare and then finished by saying 'Ah! So the bird finally decided to leave its cage and fly! Do I still bow to you?'

That was cheeky. Michael was always a wise counsellor to me, and with my permission he had rattled my cage and foundations continuously. He had also been the first person to point out the very subtle pride that I had about public speaking.

Michael and I sat and chatted about my future, work and marriage. He gave his usual humorous comments about girls, as he had done when I was a *swami*. After a while his tone changed, and with some concern he said, 'What are you going to do, Rahil?' He liked my new name. 'You can't stay in a hotel forever!'

He was right. 'I know, Michael. Right now I'm just resting and refreshing.'

He understood, but as he stood up to leave, he made an interesting statement. 'You know, Rahil, you have left one cage only to enter into a much bigger one? This world will now be your new cage.'

I understood what he meant. I knew *swamis* who had left Guruji in the past had felt a similar euphoria for a while, but when the challenges of worldly living began to take control of their lives, the *swamis* felt just as strangled as they did before.

Michael made a lot of sense, but my heart didn't agree. I had no idea how, but I just knew that I would not succumb to the pressures of the world as he and others knew it. I believed it was a myth that people accepted without thinking.

As Michael left, he asked me to keep in touch. We shook hands and I went back to my comfy sofa. I closed my eyes as the fire crackled beside me, and reflected on the space and time suddenly made available to me, just to sit by the hotel fireplace without anyone waiting on me or hoping to fetch something I hadn't asked for. Nobody watching or wondering what I was doing or thinking.

I thought of Raj and wondered what he would be going through at that moment. The questions and queries could be quite overwhelming for him. The excitement of my bold step was obscuring the fact that I would never be able to speak to him again. Somehow I accepted that truth as the normal way of life, and yet it did nag at me.

I knew that slowly I'd have to build a whole new social circle for myself. It was exciting as well as daunting, as I had no clue how that would happen. In a month's time I would be 40 and I had no idea who I'd celebrate with.

Manish and Bhavesh were quite impressed with the way I immediately integrated into society. The speed and comfort with which I made friends in local bars and cafés was remarkable to them, although I found it quite normal and easy. I didn't realise that these friendships would eventually have to be based upon a platform with substance. Operating as I was from a heart of isolation while making others feel good was not the way to hold on to relationships and friends. I had developed a skill to begin a conversation with anyone and everyone over the years, but I didn't know that deep, intimate friendships were not made from a gifted skill set.

As I entered my second week of exploration, I began to feel a little itchy about work and a career. I made a phone call to an old friend, Humphrey Walters. Humphrey had sailed around the world and written a book called *Global Challenge*. He was an incredible life coach with 5,000 people working for him, and his training and teaching had helped many top football and cricket clubs win major tournaments around the world. He was a humble and authentic man who had always had time for me over the years with his precious guidance.

We sat together for tea and he smiled. 'I knew you would leave those robes one day.'

I smiled back. 'Did you?'

'Rahil, you have such an inquisitive mind. It was sad to see you locked up in that small environment.'

I was amazed at the way he had kept it all quiet. 'Humphrey, now I need a way forward. I'm done with everything spiritual. I'm parking that side of my life now. I just want a simple life, a simple job and a wonderful marriage. I'm done with my search for God.'

He looked at me for a few seconds and gave a father-like smile. He was in his fifties and carried a wisdom that was comforting. He pulled across a piece of paper and took out his pen. 'So! What are we going to do?' he said in his humble and kind voice.

'Well, I need a curriculum vitae of some sort so that I can start to apply for jobs.'

'Rahil, 20 years of your work as a *swami* with all that travel on one CV? It's not going to be easy.'

I understood his point. Working as I had done without any pay was something the world would find difficult to grasp. All the exposure to travel, people, administration and management in the setting I had been in was very unusual. So to expect a role of the same calibre would be too ambitious. I said that I'd like to do something simple after such an intense lifestyle. We sat there with our tea and wrote down some good points, after which I began to apply for jobs in museums, art galleries and other places I had an interest in.

Day and night after that sitting with Humphrey I tried very hard for the jobs I liked the look of, but they were not coming through. I could have joined his company, but owing to his wife's health he was actually winding everything down. I didn't feel it was the right time to be with him, either, as I had just climbed out of a similar role of 'life coaching'!

Chapter 23
The end of a search

As I tried to find jobs, I continued to roam around London and enjoy my 'time out'. Spirituality was no longer on my radar. I wasn't seeking God any more. I was done with that search and frankly fed up with the whole thing. No *puja*, and nothing whatsoever of any kind of spiritual reading. I decided to do nothing with that sphere of life, as I had been very disappointed and let down by Guruji and the God I had been hoping to find. I desperately wanted a quiet and peaceful life with no doctrine, philosophy or complication.

It was with this very casual approach to life and spiritual ideas that I was walking to South Kensington station one Sunday morning. It was three or four weeks into January 2012. I was crossing Bute Street near the Zetland Arms pub, along the Old Brompton Road. Just as I was crossing, unintentionally I glanced to the right and saw a beautiful church further down the road on Sumner Place.

I stopped in my tracks and thought that it would be nice to pay a visit as I had done previously in other churches. By this time I had forgotten all of my moments and encounters with this secret God whom I didn't even know. The hurt had wiped everything out of my mind, and I didn't want to look for God anyway. Somehow my feet began to walk in the direction of this old Anglican church. Staring at the beautiful spire I thought that the church would be quiet and so it would give me some time to ponder over matters. I calculated that I'd sit for a little while and then make a move towards my initial destination.

As I came to the main entrance it was 11.15am, and to my complete surprise I saw the most unique and genuine smiles waiting at the door to welcome me in. I had never seen such radiant faces in my entire life. They greeted me and I walked through the double red doors. I didn't know that my next few footsteps would change the course of my life forever.

As I stepped through the next set of doors, suddenly a blanket of incredible peace fell on me. A peace I had never known, a peace I had worked so hard for but could never actually find, a peace that had no explanation behind it. I was baffled and stood there in the entrance for a few seconds in wonder, rooted to the spot. I couldn't comprehend the depth of this presence or even place it in a box. It felt so good.

In those few seconds that same silent voice, like years before, spoke into my left ear, gentle and honest as ever, 'You're home...'

I don't know why or how, but I was overjoyed. I was home!

When that whispering voice said the word 'home' it felt very different to the definitions I had of homes and houses. There was a deep warmth in that sound, 'home'. Something fascinating had just captivated my heart.

After a minute or so a man approached me. 'Hi, I'm Masood!' Looking at the length of his smile he might have just eaten a banana sideways.

'I'm Rahil.' I kept it simple. Just then, a few more smiley faces joined in.

'I'm Sarah...' 'I'm Josh...' 'I'm Melanie...' 'I'm Simon...'

I couldn't process the genuine love. It was so natural. I'd never seen it ooze off people in that normal and natural way.

Again I kept it simple, 'I'm Rahil,' and quickly went upstairs and sat on my own.

This was Holy Trinity Brompton (HTB) church at Onslow Square. For the first time ever I had no reason why, but I was really enjoying myself. This was a paradox! Why and how I was so overjoyed I had no idea. The atmosphere was filled with a beautiful presence and I had never seen or heard worship with guitars and drums. The sounds were travelling right into my soul, and I could sense a deep satisfaction brewing from the pit of my stomach. It was all new to me and yet I didn't find anything weird or strange. Everything sat in rhythm with my heart, and after years of searching I finally felt nourished, filled and fed. The sermon made more sense the more I listened and I didn't need to wrack my brain around any of it or figure it out.

Once the service ended, I was keen to receive prayer but I was too shy. I quietly slipped out of the main doors. As I walked back up Sumner Place I was overjoyed with the whole meeting and I remember secretly saying 'yes' in agreement to everything that had just happened.

I changed my plan of going to the next place and instead went straight back to the hotel. With a radiant smile on my face I opened the door of my heart and said yes to Jesus Christ. Months later I would realise that He was the 'Something', the 'Somebody', the 'more', the voice, the person who had been asking questions and knocking on the door of my heart time and again, in various creative and imaginative ways, for years. Later I read Jesus' words, 'Here I am! I stand at the door and knock. If anyone hears my voice and opens the door, I will come in and eat with that person, and they with me' (Revelation 3:20). I had not been brave enough to open that door before, but on that Sunday morning, with so much grace and mercy, He attracted my attention again. He guided my footsteps and led me to a beautiful encounter. Finally, after years, I opened the door of my heart and let Him in.

As I sat in my room, I knew I had something very true and alive. It was a food that nourished me like no other. I had done so many things in my life to attain this deep satisfaction, but it never arose. That morning the Lord called me and gave it without a price, without cost, totally free.

I told Manish and some other friends that I had paid a visit to a certain church, but didn't explain my encounter. I preferred it to be a secret. The secret love affair had suddenly grown to a much greater level and had become very obvious in a profound way.

I journeyed again to the church every Sunday after that encounter and sat upstairs on my own. With this new-found love of my life I wanted no attention, no significance or limelight. All I wanted was to drink in this beautiful presence and enjoy it. I told nobody of my past and didn't have the desire to do so. Nobody preached to me or shared the good news of Jesus in any way on a one-to-one basis. It was all through His loving encounter. I needed no convincing about theology or rules. I had just encountered the Living God in Jesus Christ, pure and full of love. I had met the love I had been seeking all my life.

Over the weeks, this pattern of attending the HTB church every Sunday became normal for me, but matters with Manish were beginning to go backwards. For various reasons the friendship was fracturing and I was eventually asked to leave the hotel. Thankfully, by this time another friend, Vijay, kindly offered me a job in his advertising company, and Manish was kind enough to set me up in a smart studio apartment in London's Paddington area. Manish tried his best to help me; he was a remarkable man who had stood by me when I had nowhere to go.

It was an amicable separation, and a few months later I understood why it had to be so. Moving out brought me to the next step of living on my own and supporting myself. A job and a home were now in hand.

Vijay had never been an ardent follower of Guruji. We had met infrequently and yet we had a good connection whenever we did. Over the years we shared the same out-of-the-box thinking. We had similar interests, so each time we met we sat for hours together. Vijay was quietly happy that I had left the organisation. He always hoped for the best for me and wanted me to progress in every way. He ran his company very well, but its dynamics were challenging for me. I was struggling with the whole culture of the company, as brilliant as it was. I wasn't accustomed to so much swearing and the very pushy marketing. We were chatting in his office one time about the challenges I faced. Vijay was kind and understood that I had just arrived from a very different set-up. As I was leaving the office, he gently asked me, 'Are you now a Christian?'

Somehow he was aware that I was attending church every Sunday. I stopped for a second. I had been attending church for three months by now. 'Yes,' I said.

'That's good,' he said. 'You can fill the void of not having Guruji with Christianity. One takes the place of the other.'

'Not really,' I said. 'There was already a void with Guruji. There was always something missing. The satisfaction with Guruji was only through recognition and special attention. Now, it's finally being filled with Jesus.'

I knew what Vijay was trying to say. He thought that it was always good to have some sort of faith by your side. He was trying to tell me that I had replaced one 'system' or 'structure' with another, and that I would find it difficult without an institution of some sort over me. He was wrong. I had always been aware of the effects of institutionalised religion in every area of life, even though I had been fearful of departing from one.

This journey was the beginning of a relationship with a living God, not a religion of rules and regulations like the one I had come from. This was a God who showed His generous love when He gave Jesus to die for my sin. Whatever mistake I had made that day – or tomorrow – He would go on loving me increasingly. However, I didn't try to argue with Vijay and thanked him as I left.

Other friends were concerned about my entry into the church, but they didn't make it clear to me then. This handful of close associates that reminded me of my whole life story was all that I had left, my only reference point. They were the only people now who knew my journey and my struggles, and I felt I could trust them. Suddenly, however, within a matter of weeks, during April 2012, one by one they all stopped communication. I didn't know why. I would call them and there would be no answer. I sent text messages and there was no reply. It was strange and abrupt.

Around the time of this sudden change with my friends, a vivid moment in my Paddington studio explained very clearly what was happening to everything linked to my past. One very warm evening I was ironing my shirts with my face to the wall. Behind me on the other side of the room I had placed my iPod on a glass that was filled with water. It was perfectly balanced with enough space at both ends so that it had no chance to slip into the water.

I'm not sure how or why I placed it like that as I never take such risks, even though its position made it impossible to slip into the water, or on to the table, for that matter. It was a quiet evening and not much was running through my mind. After some time, I had a weird prompting to turn around. Just then, to my shock and surprise, I saw my iPod slowly slide across the top of the glass and fall into the water! It was the most bizarre scene I had ever encountered – as if somebody slowly slid it along so that it intentionally dropped in the water. I ran to pull the soaked machine out of the full glass, but it was too late. The screen was all foggy and the machine wouldn't start.

Here I stood with this supernatural scenario, completely baffled. Interestingly, the iPod had a few speeches of Guruji's I had kept, along with my music. Even though I had given my heart to Jesus, I had felt that I should keep something of Guruji in remembrance. Now it was obviously not to be the case, as I had no backup anywhere. Guruji had finally left my life completely and forever.

I took my machine to the Apple store on London's Regent Street, and as the assistant looked down at it he said in his apologetic voice, 'Sir, it's all over!'

His words had a deeper meaning beyond the machine being broken. Every subtle strand or link to the organisation was supernaturally being severed, along with friends and now Guruji.

I believe that my iPod didn't just slip accidentally into the water but that an angel initiated it. I'm sure the idea of angels raises eyebrows for many, but by this time in my journey with Jesus it wasn't difficult for me to comprehend. It's strange, as I had seen so many supernatural incidents as a *swami* but thought that they were all matters of one's own mind and interpretation. It surprises me that I grasped the supernatural so quickly and easily when I had been so cynical and sceptical about it for years.

My hunger for the presence of Jesus grew week after week. By now I had started attending three worship services on a Sunday and yet I was still hungry for more. I wanted to know more about His love and forgiveness, and each week I drank it in. I had been in a desert for 40 years of my life and now I had a river of living water in Christ who was quenching my thirst, which enticed me to drink more and more. I realised how thirsty

I was, and the truth of His words, 'Let anyone who is thirsty come to me and drink. Whoever believes in me, as Scripture has said, rivers of living water will flow from within them' (John 7:37–38). I would learn more about that river before long.

Chapter 24
Reconnection

As this beautiful journey with Jesus continued, I knew it was time to pay a short visit to see my parents, who were still abroad. I knew that it would be very awkward. I had a new faith, and I had left all other connections behind me, so surely they would ask me a thousand questions regarding so many matters. The enormity of not having seen my parents for 20 years was something I had not thought about until it was right on my doorstep. I had no idea what I would say or do when I met them in that first moment.

I booked my ticket and informed my friends Masood, Simon and Melanie that I would be back in a few days. I had known them a very short while, but they carried a beautiful love of Jesus that was difficult to leave behind.

On the flight, I tried to picture what my parents' faces would look like. They would have aged so much since I had last seen them in 1991. I had no idea what had happened in their life during those years whilst I was in orange robes. What the extended family was doing and the financial situation of everyone were completely out of my grid. I had been cut off from the whole family for far too long. My brain was getting stressed, so I turned on the news that was giving an update of the 2012 Olympic Games in London.

I tried to divert my mind and fall asleep, but by the time I felt a little drowsy we were landing. As I wheeled my trolley out of the arrivals area, my heart began to race as I tried to think what my parents' faces would look like. Eventually I spotted them and they met my gaze with a smile. I was in an emotional mix and I had no clue what to say or where to start.

'Hello!' was all that tumbled out my mouth. It was an awful effort that made me even more uncomfortable, especially as I had run away from them all those years ago. Thankfully I didn't say, 'I'm back again!' That would have been a disaster.

Dad was awesome and smooth and he jumped in straight away to break the silence. 'Son! How are you? It's been a while.'

His face had a beaming smile which suggested his utmost pride and joy in seeing me. Dad will always be Dad, I thought. Never failing to give me hope. I tried not to cry. I didn't want him to see the disappointment I had with the way my life had panned out. He was very calm and stable as ever. It was as if I had never vanished from his life at all. Dad had seen many storms in his life since the day his father had died, and yet I've seen him time and again maintain a wonderful sense of composure.

Mum burst into tears as soon as I gave her a hug. She didn't let me go for a while. I couldn't bear it for too long, so I eventually let go of her, but Mum being Mum continued her flood of tears. We sat in the car and made our way home. My initial impression was that they had chosen to live a very simple and peaceful life far away from the stresses and strains of London. My stay was very restful. We went on long walks together and talked for hours, trying to catch up with all the news of our long, meandering, individual lives.

Dad was very relaxed about my desire to journey with Jesus, but I could see his face suggesting, 'Oh, no, son. Not again! You just came out of one faith and so quickly you're getting into another?'

This altered over time, and eventually, when he noticed the change in me, he became very proud and honoured Jesus with a deep respect. My mother, however, was always tough to deal with – for me, anyway. We had a very challenging time with each other. At one stage we even raised our voices to each other. That was expected so it didn't disturb me. At the same time she couldn't resist pampering and hugging me. 'You look very smart, son,' she said one afternoon during lunch, and then very quickly delivered the typical Patel punchline, 'When are you getting married?' I laughed and said it was too early for that.

Overall, we had some quality time together and ate very good food. My mum cooked the most delicious meals for me and I enjoyed every one. After all those years, her food was still the best ever, and I was sure that she was the best cook in the world. As I took my first bite I realised how much I had missed her food, and it was a very emotional moment.

I sat there one evening pondering how difficult it must have been for both my parents not to have seen me for 20 years. I couldn't fathom what they had been through, and it hurt me quite a bit to think what I had done to them. One afternoon during a meal in a restaurant I looked at them, ashamed, and said, 'I'm sorry I abandoned you and ran away.'

Mum was silent and Dad, typically, replied, 'That's fine, son.'

I had missed them too. Dad had sent me a secret letter when I was stationed in Mumbai and I remembered the words well. 'Son, there is no love lost from us. We wish you all the best…' I had read that letter several times and couldn't hold back my tears. I had kept it hidden in my drawer so that nobody could find it.

It was a fruitful two weeks with Mum and Dad, and yet not always comfortable. It was very difficult to connect at certain levels, as we had limited time to know what had happened in each other's lives. I had not been allowed by Guruji's rules to communicate with them, and neither had they been allowed to enter into my life. It was very sad to reflect that from now on the same thing would apply between myself and Raj. I would not know anything about his life after 40 years of friendship, and neither would he know what was happening in mine.

I had a very early morning flight back to London and Dad gladly came to drop me off at the airport. Mum was very tired and so I asked her not to come. From now on we would slowly build upon the relationship in the best way possible. But for now it was farewell as I boarded my flight, and so I gave Dad a hug and promised to stay in touch.

I fastened my seat belt and stared out of the window in my usual way. I already missed them both. I closed my eyes and said a small prayer to Jesus to protect their lives and hopefully bring Raj home one day so that he could encounter the true living God as I had. Eventually, I fell asleep.

Chapter 25
Stripping away

London brought me back to the rhythm of work, home and church.

Simon and Melanie Stanton were my house-group leaders within the church. I attended their small group every Tuesday. Simon phoned me the day after I returned from seeing my parents and said, 'Rahil, we have put your name down for the Alpha course.' I was still slightly jet-lagged and yet I was excited to begin the ten-week course.

Alpha is a wonderful course initiated by HTB that runs all over the world and has helped to bring clarity to believers and non-believers on the person of Jesus. It explores with very open discussions truths about the cross, the resurrection and the person of the Holy Spirit. It's open to anyone who is interested in finding out more about Jesus, regardless of their faith background.

The course started in May and I began to enjoy it, with the open discussions and, of course, the great food! It gave me a good overall view about the life of Jesus and His ministry. I understood more clearly what He had done for me. It wasn't only His amazing teaching, which He lived out completely. It was also His dying, not just as an example of love, but also as a sacrifice to deal with our deepest needs and open the way back to God.

Though I was attending Sunday services and midweek groups I still didn't have an idea of what a Christian community and 'family' felt like. Sharing my heart with vulnerability was something unknown to me, and very alien. I went to house-group meetings but mostly sat there and listened. I seldom asked for prayer as I never shared with anybody matters of my past, or my current journey with regard to my work and career. I felt very ashamed about my past and somehow hoped that nobody would ever know about it.

Because of my hurts, I was also keeping my heart in a gridlock. I wasn't going to lend it out any more as I had done with Guruji, Raj and my close friends. Nobody was allowed close to my heart and I made sure of that, so that I would never be hurt again. I shifted my boundaries with great caution so that people would gain minimum access to my life. Owing to the kindness of people such as Masood, Simon and Melanie I wasn't pushed with questions. Looking back, it was helpful that I had that space and time before I opened up my heart again.

Work was becoming more and more challenging as the environment was very intense. I had just come from a very intense place and my heart was still very sore. Vijay noticed and was very kind and understanding. He could see that I was uncomfortable, and so he was gentle and suggestive as to how I should manoeuvre. It was a commission-based job and I wasn't doing well at all. In fact, I was hopeless. My heart and mind were not present as deeper issues of resentment and bitterness were now erupting during my day. Hatred for Guruji and the organisation was surfacing, and I just could not concentrate.

Honestly, by the end of August 2012 I was panicking as to how my life would pan out. I still had no money except for food. I had a studio that needed the rent to be paid and I was beginning to go into arrears. I was getting desperate to make a shift in my life and here I admit that after my first few months of free time, wandering and enjoying the fresh air, my desire to prove myself and perform crept to the surface again. I was still very restless underneath, although I had had an eye-opening encounter with Jesus. I was still very bitter, very resentful and very angry with everyone in my life, as well as myself. There was a deeply rooted hatred sitting dormant underneath. I didn't want anyone's advice or anyone to tell me what to do. I just wanted to be established with my own efforts, my own hard work.

At this point my dad offered to give me money to start my own business. He was expecting a large sum from a transaction that was on the verge of completion. It looked very promising. I said yes in my frantic restlessness. He was my dad and I knew I could trust him. He told me to leave my job, as the money would be in my bank within a week. I would have trod with caution if it were somebody else, but he was my dad, after all. I spoke to Vijay who was shocked at my decision, as we were good friends.

'Why would you want to leave now? Let's work a bit more as I'm hoping you can earn enough to buy a house one day.'

Vijay was wise and he was a little unsure about the sum my dad had promised me. But I wasn't going to listen and eventually, in my passion for performance, I jumped from his company. Vijay was sad and felt that he couldn't stop me. I felt that he was unnecessarily sceptical and was preventing me from taking an easier route that would propel me forward, when I was so far behind at my age. Sadly, we had an argument and the friendship cracked quite severely. He and I no longer communicated after that.

I was contemplating what I would do with the incoming money and sat proudly in the beautiful Kensington Gardens viewing the fountains. I knew where I'd buy my home and who

I would ask to advise me with investment. I made my to-do list and was excited. I was going to show people that I wasn't a loser.

However, after a day or so I was gripped with fear and began to doubt. I phoned my father, who calmed me down by saying that there were a few delays. I wasn't convinced but I still trusted him, so I waited. I had enough money to buy food for a few more days. I still had my studio and there was time to pay the rent. But then three days, four days, and no sign of the money.

'I told you a week, so please be patient!' he said.

I was really trembling. My anxiety increased and I couldn't sleep. I had left my job and with that Vijay's friendship, and by now Manish was no longer in my life.

What will I do? I thought. On the seventh day I called him again. He didn't pick up. I tried every half hour and he just wouldn't pick up the phone. Three days later I managed to get through to him and we had a huge argument over the phone, after which he said that the deal he was managing had not gone through and so there was no money. My heart just about stopped. I asked him in a frank and fair manner how that came about, as he had been so sure. At the end of my questioning he admitted that there had been nothing definite from the very start.

'Why did you ask me to leave my job?' I asked.

He had no answer. I raised my voice, to which he shouted back, 'Well, you should not have run away all those years ago!'

I was devastated and so confused. I couldn't believe my ears. My own father and friend who I felt understood me and loved me had left me in the most desperate circumstances. I had just shared with him during my recent visit how I had been let down by Guruji after serving him for 20 years, and now he had done the same.

Looking back, I feel my dad was desperate to help me gain a footing as he knew I had nothing to my name after so many years. In his deep desire as a dad to keep my hopes high, he lost sight of the consequences if his promises didn't come through. The consequences were dire.

In my desperation for quick money I had acted unwisely, and now I was absolutely stuck. What would I do now? Where could I go? I had no food left and no money to buy more. I had a handful of oranges that I ate over three days. That was all.

I decided to go to the pastorate that summer evening, and as the bus stopped by the Moravian Chapel on the King's Road, the driver kindly waited until I could get some money for the fare. I ran inside and met Masood.

'I've forgotten my Oyster card and need a little money, so would you help?'

'Sure,' he said.

I didn't know how to reveal what was going on in my life outside of church – and I didn't want to, either. So I had lied to him. I ran back and gave the money to the driver.

I came back in and Masood was rehearsing some worship songs on his guitar. I was crushed under the whole situation. My ability and capacity to trust had vanished. That day I decided that I would never trust anyone ever again. After what I had experienced, I had felt I had a few close friends left whom I could trust and they fell through, and then my own dad...

I thought again about what he had done, whatever good motive there might have been. It dawned on me that in my own life I had made many empty promises to people around me as well. I had convinced people about ideas and matters relating to God that I myself didn't believe. In effect, I was letting people down. I saw that I had done similar things in different situations and realised that I was not to be trusted, either. The thought sickened me.

I sat and pondered all those people I had helped for all those years, attending to each individual's problems late into the night. All those homes I had visited in Europe and London when my body had been so tired and ill. Those phone calls to solve family disputes, and meetings to settle divorces. What was it all for? Is this where it had led me? I even looked back at the accusations made about me when I left. People claimed that I left with a lot of money. People I thought were friends made up lies about my character and my departure. I was completely broken.

Masood looked at me and said, 'You alright, mate?'

A gush of tears ran down my cheeks.

'What's wrong?' He stopped rehearsing and took me into the dining area where a few others were seated. I sat there and narrated the whole situation. Along with Melanie and Simon, he listened with the utmost compassion while I gave a brief history of where I was from and how I had ended up in a situation without food for three days.

Masood was shocked. 'That is unacceptable, Rahil! Why didn't you say anything?'

I was stunned by the question. The best I could say was, 'I never knew I could share my problems.'

Later in my journey with Christ, I realised where that belief about not sharing my heart had come from. Holding every issue and problem inside, burying it or trying to solve it myself, was something I had learned over years. His question was so new to me.

'Rahil, in the kingdom we are a family who love and share our problems. Love is a sacrifice.'

Melanie fed me and then Masood gave me his office address and asked me to meet him the next day.

The next morning I took the bus to Masood's office in Mayfair. I was stressed and worried and as simple as his address was to find, I walked in circles for a while. Finally, I found Queen Street, and as I walked towards his office I passed a beautiful gentlemen's grooming salon by the name of George F. Trumper. Gone were the days of shopping in such beautiful places, as now

I was about to be homeless. I shook off the thought of such nice things and entered Masood's office.

Masood had come from a Muslim background. His family had disowned him completely when he gave his life to Jesus and so the church, the body of Christ, had become his family. He had a very humble beginning in his financial business and so money was in short supply. Despite his own situation being so dire at the time, he took me to his local bank and cashed £1,000 from his personal account. I found out much later that that was all he had in his savings – with a family of four to feed. He handed me a pile of £50 notes, and with a genuine smile said, 'Eat! I want you to eat to your heart's content.'

I couldn't comprehend what he was saying, so I followed my usual tendency and asked, 'Would you like me to tell you where I've spent it?'

'No, it's yours now!'

This was so new to me. How could he give me money and not want to know where and how I would spend it?

He said with a laugh, 'I've given it to you and so now it's yours. It's no longer mine and so spend it how you want!'

This was too much for me to balance in my brain. 'Giving' from my experience had a very monitored approach. I had seen people give money in my life – vast sums – and yet there were always certain strings attached. But this was unconditional giving from an unconditional heart.

As I placed the money in my pocket I realised that I had some serious unlearning to do. I had suddenly been made aware of a journey that required the reshaping of my heart. With my background, that was an area always ignored or suppressed. From this very early encounter of unconditional love, Masood became a very close friend who helped me settle in so many ways. He was a Godsend.

The following day, I used some of the money to travel to Manchester to attend a conference with other followers of Christ from South Asian backgrounds. One of them helped me make a new CV on the train journey back. I started to distribute my second CV from Masood's office in Mayfair. It was an endless affair. I walked and walked in the search for jobs, and at each juncture I was told that there was nothing.

Meanwhile, September 2012 was my ninth month of journeying with Christ. I had a desire to be baptised in water. It would be a very special time of public commitment. During that week I noticed some of the distractions I would face on my journey. I was told to vacate my studio in Paddington as I couldn't pay the rent, and so I was about to become homeless. I had no idea what to do or where to go.

Strangely, for the first time in my life, in the midst of this suffering I felt a joy which knew no bounds, as I was publicly announcing my faith in Jesus. I was so happy and proud. There were 12 of us and I still remember going under the water at HTB Onslow Square on that beautiful Sunday evening.

'Rahil, I baptise you in the name…'

Then I was under and up again, buried and resurrected with Christ. It was a symbol of my sins being washed away and then beginning a new life. After the baptism I shared a brief testimony of my background. The congregation was amazed at the way that Jesus had pulled me into His kingdom.

After that wonderful and jubilant event, my job search continued at a sluggish pace. I delivered CVs in the Mayfair area near Masood's office and anywhere else I could. Bookshops, art galleries, hotels and antique shops… But I was still stressed and having several panic attacks a day. At times I would suddenly begin to walk fast, unaware of what I was running from. I was depressed and yet strangely still passionate for Jesus. There was no rationale, in the natural sense, for why I was pursuing Him in this way; there was no guru to tell me or any structure to push me through fear. It was my choice, and I wanted Him more and more in my heart.

Chapter 26
A deep filling

During the month of October, when I was in a season of complete and utter stripping away of everything, the most incredible incident took place. I was asleep on the sofa in Masood's office one evening, feeling sad and downcast. After a while he woke me up and said, 'Hey Rahil! Go to Happy Hour at GIM tonight! C'mon, get off that sofa and get going. I'll see you there later.' (Growing in Ministry is a prophetic ministry at HTB run by a lovely man called Mark Wagner.)

'Happy Hour? You've got to be kidding me! What is Happy Hour?'

'Just go! I'll see you when the main meeting starts.'

'Fine.' I took the bus and ended up in the HTB 24/7 prayer room where Happy Hour was running. Five people were present.

Two women, Miriam and Elise, were running the hour of worship. Before the worship began, Miriam said, 'Move around a bit so that the Lord's Spirit can move in you.'

I understood what she was saying, but I was reluctant to dance or 'move around' as she said. So I had my eyes closed during worship and stood like a rock, upright and stiff as ever! I opened my eyes a little as Elise began to dance around all of us. As she passed by me, she laid a finger on my chest. At that moment, to my shock, surprise and joy, I felt a small river deep in my stomach beginning to flow! It was tiny and moving up to my chest. I didn't force it and definitely never imagined it. As the river rose above and through my chest, a deep and satisfying laughter broke out of me. I've seen laughter classes throughout the world, and I had read about them, too. It wasn't that forced-up laughter you hear about in those classes; rather, it had a natural, beautiful and authentic flow. It wasn't mine and it felt very nourishing. This was the 'river of living water' that Jesus spoke about, referring to 'the Spirit, whom those who believed in him were later to receive' (John 7:39).

I didn't expect it and never knew it existed. My countenance and mood changed within seconds. The person next to me said, 'You look way different than you did when you came in.'

True! I knew it. I *felt* different. My mind felt so settled. 'What was that? How did that happen? A river? Inside of me?'

My hunger suddenly went to another level. Jesus Christ was even more real than I had thought. The truth that He is alive became physically tangible to me within seconds. I had received the baptism of the Holy Spirit. I was experiencing what Jesus' follower Paul prayed for: 'that ... he may strengthen you with power through his Spirit in your inner being, so that Christ may dwell in your hearts through faith ... being rooted and established in love' (Ephesians 3:16–17).

I was now on fire! I wanted more and more of what had just happened. I felt so nourished and fed. It was much stronger and deeper than the day I had first walked into church that Sunday morning. I was prepared to pay the price now. Whatever the cost, I didn't care, and I wanted more of Jesus.

My friends were amazed that in such a short time a radical transformation was beginning to take place, and they were so excited. Joy had entered my house as never before. My inner temple was filled and my spirit had a union with His. It was the Lord's joy, a celebration in my heart.

I then recalled all those readings and meditations by Aurobindo and other gurus and leaders. They were trying hard to awaken their souls, seeking for their souls to break through and override their bodies and their ego. But here was the power that they needed, the baptism and fullness of the Spirit of Jesus. When I responded to Jesus to receive His love and forgiveness, He entered into my life by His Spirit. Now I experienced the joy and power of His presence. I realised I had found what they were seeking.

That night my perception changed drastically. Although I still struggled with no job, money or place to live, I was infused with a purpose. Life suddenly meant something. I was living for Someone who radically loved me and gave Himself for me – Jesus. I knew that my destiny and purpose was to pursue His Presence. All of my needs would be met there.

Masood was overjoyed at my encounter, and the next day we met again at his office to look for simple rooms for me to stay in. I had a day or two left in my Paddington home and Masood reassured me that God would provide.

'Rahil, He is *Jehovah-jireh*. That is His name which means "The Lord will provide". He always provides and will never let you down.'

It was another learning curve for me. I was so used to having everything planned in my own strength, in order to secure my safety and needs, and here the Lord began to teach me how to trust Him as a Father. I found that very difficult, as my earthly father had let me down. So to believe that God was my Father took me through a struggling inner journey of trust and surrender.

At the very last minute, we found a flatshare in Brixton and I was very thankful. God had provided and didn't let me down.

This was the first of many incidents that happened where I had to learn to trust Him as a good Father who would provide for all my needs.

It was a simple room on the ground floor, and the landlord was a kind fellow who let me stay for a full month even though I didn't have a job. 'You will find one!' he said. 'The Lord will provide!' He was a member of a local church and continued to give me encouragement.

I sold whatever I had to pay for the deposit. Masood, Melanie, Simon and a few others gave some money for the deposit as well. So I had a place to live and rest. Slowly, although with difficulty, matters were falling into place. One more stress was off the list.

During this time of not having a job and minimum money to buy basic food, I remember my journey home one night on the bus. I was leaning against the window on the upper deck, pondering the huge challenges and difficulties in my first year of leaving the orange robes. I looked at the river as the bus moved south, and a thought came into my mind.

In just ten months, the love of Jesus had overlapped everything I had had for 20 years as a *swami*. All the recognition, the attention, the adoration, the worship, the affirmation from Guruji, and all the luxury. Now I had nothing to my name and no frills in my life, but the encounter with the living God was worth even more and beautifully overwhelming. I was not turning back. Not because I had nothing to go back to. I could have gone back to some friends in the organisation and asked for help, but the attraction of Christ was all-consuming. His love was the comfort and nourishment I had craved all my life. That void deep in my soul was now beginning to be filled by His Spirit.

I'm all in this now, I thought. My search was over: my desperate readings and meditations, my temple pilgrimages and rituals, my *pujas* and *artis*. They all added up to nothing compared to the manifest tangible presence of Jesus Christ. They were all about 'doing' to achieve some peace and find some internal transformation. Now it had all been 'done' without effort, just by His love. He had forgiven me, washed me clean and given me new life. Jesus' follower Paul expressed it so clearly: 'it is by grace you have been saved, through faith – and this is not from yourselves, it is the gift of God' (Ephesians 2:8).

No self-help theory was needed now as I began to notice the change from within. My physical body as well as my behaviour were beginning to change. It was a mind-blowing miracle. Finally God had come to me and rested beautifully in my heart. I smiled as the bus took me home.

Soon after I arrived in Brixton I went to the Ruach Church where my landlord was a member. It was very new to me and so I felt a little awkward. The pastor was a lovely African lady. At the end she gave a prophetic word to the whole congregation: 'From this day in four weeks' time, there will be a miracle.'

I knew that word was for me and that God had a specific job lined up for me. After receiving the word, I had another encounter similar to the one in Happy Hour. I went home filled with joy, and waited for the Lord to come through on His promise.

During this time I managed to complete the full Alpha course again, including the Holy Spirit weekend. A number of different Alpha groups travelled together to the coast for a weekend and received further teaching and insight on the Holy Spirit. At this wonderful time, one of the curates suggested that we all ask the Holy Spirit for the gift of tongues. This is a heavenly language and biblically rooted. It's a beautiful way to pray or worship when we are unsure what to pray for. It's a powerful way to engage with His Spirit and brings a lot of strength to one's own spirit.

I stood there thinking that it would be nice to have that gift. The worship began and people around me began to sing in tongues. The sound was heavenly and beautiful. It connected my spirit with the Lord's. Just then, out of my heart a heavenly language flowed with the most wonderful sound and feeling. I was amazed that God just gave me the gift. Something that I thought would take years of prayer and petition came in an instant. I realised that my God was a God of the impossible.

I sat down in my chair and streams of tears, with a deep satisfaction, ran down my cheeks. The love flowing from heaven was overwhelming and I allowed it to heal my hurts.

After the evening session was over, I had a wonderful chat with David Walker, one of the vicars at HTB. A month earlier he had given a powerful talk on the importance of vulnerability in community and I had been touched quite deeply. As we sat together that night, David shared how one can be surrounded by hundreds of people and yet feel very lonely. I knew that feeling very well – years of it! We decided to meet and pray about this area in my life, as I was aware of the walls I had placed around my heart to protect it. David became a solid and consistent friend in my life, always ready to talk, help and pray.

The weekend was over and we travelled back to London. God had given me some wonderful friends who were passionate for Jesus. He began to fulfil another promise: that I would never be without friends. As I travelled home that night I smiled as I thought of a time when I wondered how I would build a whole new social circle again. I didn't have to do anything – my heavenly Father was providing them. He was sending godly people into my life to love me, to guide me and to have fun with.

The next day I began my search for a job again. I knew that God had something for me and I was waiting for 31st October, as that would be exactly four weeks after I received the word in Brixton. As time went by, though, I became more and more restless and eventually the stress overtook the date and miracle I was waiting for. Totally forgetting the prophecy and the date, I was in Berkeley Square on 31st October, wandering around a bookshop and handing out my CV.

Just then my phone rang. 'Hello, is that Rahil?' It was a very kind and gentle voice.

'Yes.'

'I'm Ms Paulette Trumper-Bersch, the owner of George F. Trumper.'

With no idea what all that meant, I continued. 'Yes?'

'I believe you're looking for a job?'

'Yes.'

'You handed in a CV to my Mayfair shop a while back.'

I had totally forgotten, as I handed out stacks of CVs. But I played along. 'Yes... I did...'

'Do you have a job, Rahil?'

'No.'

'Would you like one?'

'Yes!'

'Do you know a little about my company?'

I stumbled, 'Yes.'

'Good! I'll interview you tomorrow at 4pm myself.'

'Sure!'

I put the phone down and panicked. I ran back to Masood's office, trying to figure out what in heaven's name was Trumper! I searched and realised it was the beautiful shop just a few doors from his office that I had glimpsed a month before. I remembered placing my CV there as it was a grooming salon filled with history and art. I did some research in anticipation of many questions being asked, as it dealt with very high-end clients, all from different parts of the British establishment.

The next day I went to the shop and Ms Trumper-Bersch welcomed me downstairs to the staffroom. I was ready with all my answers, but weirdly, she didn't ask me much. Within three minutes she looked at me and said, 'You have a friendly face. I would like you to work for me. Would you like that?'

My brain, as it had done all year, again went into malfunction but luckily the word came out. 'Yes!'

I tried to hold my excitement back but couldn't do so. I may have shaken her hand a little too hard.

I went back to Masood's office leaping with joy. God had promised me a job in four weeks, and even though I forgot the date, He came through again and delivered His promise.

Very quickly I realised why the Lord gave me that job. It was peaceful and quiet. The clients and my co-workers were all very pleasant. Geo. F. Trumper is a British establishment that dates back to 1875. Trumper himself was the official barber to King George VI and he made bespoke perfumes and shaving products for gentlemen across the Royal Family, Military and Parliament. It then extended itself to the law courts and banks and is now world famous with its two shops in Mayfair and St James's.

The greatest blessing from God in this place of work was the area manager, Kamil. He became a dear friend very quickly who helped, like others, to rebuild my life and support all my involvement in the church and various ministries. He knew that my background was rather unusual, as so many things didn't add up for him. But he didn't ask or probe. Eventually I told him my story and it touched his heart. After that day he began to support my journey in Christ more and more.

The Trumper family literally became a family to me and I realised that God knew exactly what type of people I needed at this stage in my life. Going to work didn't seem like work as much as it seemed like walking into a home. I was loved in church and I was loved at work. I am so thankful that God gave me that place and all the wonderful people. It was a restful place for me to be while He carried out the deep inner healing in my heart.

By the end of 2012 I began to see that although God was stripping me of everything that wasn't from Him, He was also building me up again in His own way, step by step. He began to open my eyes to the variety of ways that He was working in my life. It was the beginning of a journey of trust, a journey of relationship with a Father who loves me unconditionally.

It was very uncomfortable, as I had come from a background of works and proving myself. It was very difficult to allow Him to move freely in my life and to provide all my needs without me trying to take over and get in His way.

So the year ended with a beautiful Christmas with Masood, Simon, Melanie and my house group. It had been a roller coaster of a year, probably the most intense thus far in my life. Deep wounds and hurts were met through powerful encounters with Christ. New friends and family were brought in by the Lord and old ones disappeared. There was a lot of change and it was very sudden. A new job and a new home added to the new life I was living.

He wasn't done, though. I knew it wasn't over. It was the beginning now of a deep healing and restoration, a journey of daily forgiveness. I knew, difficult as it was, that if I wanted more of Jesus in my heart I would have to forgive. Forgive the organisation. Forgive Guruji. Forgive my brother and parents and, more than anything, forgive myself. Only then would Christ take more space in my heart and so work from the inside out. It was very difficult for me to forgive. I was so bitter and resentful, so angry and hurt. Yet I knew He would come through and meet me where I was and rebuild my heart again. This time, shaped and carved by Him alone.

Chapter 27
The presence, discipleship and inner healing

Just after my wonderful encounter at the Happy Hour, I heard an announcement about an inner healing course called 'Salvo', which means 'to be saved, healed and delivered'. Masood turned to me and said, 'You should do that, mate.'

'What is it?' I asked.

'It's a deep prayer based on inner healing that addresses very deep wounds and hurts that we encounter in our lives from childhood. It's a biblical prayer that takes us on a journey to becoming whole in God – close to Jesus, close to the Holy Spirit, and Father God, too. A lot of your illness, Rahil, may have to do with deep wounds, hurts and trauma.'

As he was explaining, it all made sense. I agreed to join the prayer course. I attended every Monday night for ten weeks and each of them, I remember, was very uncomfortable. Wounds in my heart from the past were unearthed and lies that I had believed were discovered. These had skewed my perspective of God and my relationship with Him. The nature of the prayer course was to reveal and heal the wounds and lies so that I could continue my journey of becoming whole in God.

Near and dear friends reminded me that the Christian walk is about becoming whole in Christ. But my heart was being stirred and troubled week after week and I wanted to stop each time I left the session.

Simultaneously, I could see the deeper levels of freedom I was attaining. My view of Father God began to change as I forgave my earthly father. My relationship with the Holy Spirit developed as I forgave my earthly mother, and the same with Jesus as I forgave Raj. It was a deep and very biblical course where I was taken into various memories of my life where I needed healing.

I could forgive because I had been forgiven myself. As I went back through my memories I realised the depths of my own self-will and stubbornness that had broken my family. I had been so proud and enjoyed the flattery and adulation of others. I had put on a façade to cover my inner emptiness. I realised now how much I had grieved my heavenly Father. And yet He had given Himself, in the person of His pure Son, to suffer and die in my place. He had carried all my shame and sin and failure. There was nothing for me to do but receive His forgiveness. It was liberating. I experienced what it meant to be 'tenderhearted, forgiving one another, as God in Christ forgave you' (Ephesians 4:32, RSV).

After all the books I had read on self-help and deep inner personality dynamics, I finally came to this course that got to the root of my behaviour which was not of God. I was amazed at the immediate changes in me which I had tried to attain by myself for years but couldn't.

My date for special healing prayer arrived at the end of the snow-filled month of January. I hadn't seen so much snow in a while. I fasted for a week before my prayer, after which Masood drove me to the HTB offices on Cromwell Road opposite the Natural History Museum. I was grateful that he stood by me as

I journeyed through my inner hurts. Masood always pointed me in the right direction, but also had the steady heart to be by my side to see me through it.

After Masood drove away, two people began to lead me through my Salvo prayer. Lucy and Amelia created a very safe place for me. They led me through areas of my life and background that needed a healing touch from God. As the Holy Spirit led them I was taken to various memories from my childhood, as well as with Guruji and Raj, that needed healing. I forgave as I was led and forgave myself for many things, too, because I knew that I was forgiven. As the time went by in the quiet and peaceful office room, I felt a release and sense of freedom.

After three hours of prayer and healing, I left to go home feeling very rested and clear. A fogginess over my mind had lifted. That night I slept like a baby, a deep sleep that I had never had in 20 plus years. It was astounding, as I had taken so many drugs to sleep well over the years, and here I was with a rested soul. This was not simply some kind of counselling or psychotherapy, but a biblical prayer that addressed the hurts and wounds of the soul.

I reflected on that prayer and realised that life and deep inner healing were not going to be a quick fix but a process. I was convinced furthermore that I had found the Healer of all my deep and surface issues in the person of Jesus. He wasn't going to tell me that the body was meant for sickness like Guruji, but quietly and yet speedily heal me with a passion. I had believed that the body was meant to fall sick and so one should accept and tolerate it. But my God is the One who heals and that is His nature.

During this inner adventure, my time in Brixton was also a challenging experience. It was a buzzing hub for transport and so, for me, rather overcrowded. The home was cosy but the area was very different from where I had grown up. My learning curve had just taken another jump, as I saw people affected by drugs, drink or other needs. I had read about such situations, I had seen films and I had visited tough places – but always in a fancy car, and I never climbed out! This whole experience was a shock to my system. It was another facet of my heart journey that God wanted to work on. I was broken and yet He wanted me to witness other aspects of brokenness in the wider society.

Living on my own and shopping for food and everyday things was another learning curve. I had to think about every aspect of my day, and it was stressful. Washing clothes, drying clothes, ironing. Cleaning my room, travel card, commuting, full-time work. The worst was shopping for food and cooking!

I could tell you how much a plane ticket should cost to any destination in the world based on the time of the year. I could tell you the value of a large property, whether it was worth buying and its annual running costs. I could explain in detail the functioning of the diamond trade. But if you had asked me at that time how much I should spend on a loaf of bread, I would have been stuck and confused!

When I walked into Sainsbury's grocery store I had a very small amount to spend and a very hungry Gujarati stomach. There were times when I overspent and times when I wasted food. Either way, the finances weren't working well. Once I phoned Masood as I left the supermarket. I was so hungry that I had overspent my budget. I broke down in tears. 'How does this all work? It's so new to me!'

He replied, 'Ask the Holy Spirit to tell you what to buy.'

'What?'

This was taking conversation with God to another level. How could I ask God such a simple question? At that moment the Lord said, 'I'm your Father. You can ask Me anything, however

225

insignificant it may sound. You are My son and I care about all your needs.'

This opened my relationship with Him to a much more personal and deep level. I had never known that I could talk to God about the most simple and trivial things, but I realised then that they mattered to Him. As I walked back home, with shopping bags in my hands, He said, 'I have seen you steward hundreds of thousands of pounds well, Rahil, but I want to teach you how to steward pennies! I want you to learn, but learn from Me.'

It was a powerful moment, and very quickly, though with a lot of discomfort, I grasped His ways. My tight finances gave me insight, over time, of how many people lived their lives. I had seen and stayed with very poor people, as well as the rich, but I had never felt the pinch as I was always on the receiving end of their hospitality. I was never in a credit crunch. If I hadn't followed current affairs, I would have thought that the credit crunch was a cereal bar!

This was part of the Lord's plan to restore my relationship with Him and bring me to a place of being childlike in His eyes. Asking and telling Him everything slowly and peacefully became a very deep and refreshing journey, as I saw that He listened and delivered answers. What mattered to me mattered to Him.

As life began to settle for me in Brixton, so did the healing in my body. I was still in the process of recovery from certain illnesses, but had miraculously given up taking Clonazepam anti-depressant tablets in 2012 in an instant. It was easy and I had no side effects. It was a striking difference from the time when I had tried to give up the medication after leaving the Mayo Clinic. There was a strength that came from Jesus. It wasn't my willpower or positive thinking, but the Lord's working and grace.

In this journey of healing I didn't believe that doctors were second class or unnecessary in any way. I noticed how the Lord was directly and supernaturally healing my body as well as using doctors, and thus revealing His nature. Again, it was a relationship that He wanted, and for me to hear His voice. If He sent me to doctors for certain matters I went with a prayerful heart, and other times He would deal with the matter directly Himself.

This wasn't always easy, as I wanted a quick fix. My friend Sheila told me, 'Rahil, we don't earn God's healing. We receive it by resting in His presence.' Sitting next to her, Deborah Paul added, 'The kingdom is not about striving.' In the year ahead I was to learn more that my physical ailments were not just emotionally linked, but also spiritual.

After the Alpha weekend, David Walker and I began to meet and pray every Tuesday morning for two hours. David was a wonderful man of God, rooted in the Word and very Spirit led. We would go for walks in South Kensington after his early morning meeting at HTB, and it worked for me as it was my day off. He would begin by asking about my week and then he would ask how my heart was getting along. He had a very simple and loving way to address the questions I had. After a while we would sit on a bench and read from the Gospel of Mark and then meditate upon the verses. David would then pray for me and I would pray for him. This mentoring from such a grounded lover of the Lord every Tuesday gave me a very steady and sound platform.

I had many fears at the time about finance and food. But my main fear was that I had no reference point for my whole life's existence. I wasn't yet rooted in Christ alone. For years my identity was based upon my skills, guru, organisation, travel and all the paraphernalia linked to them. Now the spectrum of my life was no longer around me, and so there was no reference point for me to gauge my existence. For years my definition of myself had been gauged by my surroundings, the people who worshipped me and the work I did. Now all that had been taken away, and I felt that I was 'free falling'. Yes, the encounters with Christ were daily and powerful, yet there was still this fear. In the next two years that would change. God slowly drew me closer and closer and began to reveal to me that He alone was the reference point for my identity and existence.

I began to learn that God was not just present in a church or worship setting, but with me wherever I was. As the weather began to get a little warmer in March, my time with God at home became more and more enjoyable. Every morning and on my days off His presence would fall in my room as I worshipped, and so I began to enjoy time alone with Him.

This daily practice slowly began to root me and bring peace to my day. This wasn't the peace known by the world, where there is an absence of chaos. It was a real fulfilment of the desire of all Hindus for *shanti* (peace). The deep and beautiful peace of Christ overrode all my circumstances, whether it was a lack of money or not having a home of my own. It was not the 'stillness' practised by Hindu *swamis*, as I had done, but a presence, a peace filled with His love and from Him directly. That peace and the comfort of being loved by a Father was reaching straight to my soul and brought more and more rest as the days went by. It was not conjured up but given without any effort, all by His grace and mercy.

I kept thinking of Raj at this time, and wondered what he would say if he were to taste the God I was enjoying. I couldn't have any connection with him, but I was able to connect with my dad again and we stayed in touch regularly by email and phone from then on.

A brief meeting with Ravi Zacharias in April led to another aspect which I needed to unlearn. Ravi is a brilliant apologist, who speaks all over the world. His team offered me a bursary to do a course in apologetics at his centre in Oxford. I was excited and very drawn to the idea, but my reasons were not healthy. I was striving and still in the pattern of 'What can I do for God?' I had come from a very intellectual background of study devoid of any relationship with God. I still had these intellectual strongholds that wanted to figure out God, His ways and patterns. It was another aspect of keeping busy and justifying my existence.

David and I sat one morning in a coffee shop opposite HTB and prayed about the idea. His wise advice made so much sense. 'Rahil, your entering into the kingdom has been through an encounter with God's love. At this point in time you may not want to place so much intellectual scaffolding around it. Keep receiving His love, and develop a relationship until it becomes a lifestyle, and then maybe a deep study of the Bible would be better.'

He was right, as I was striving, even though it sounded spiritual. Sitting and 'being' was very new to me as I had been entrenched in 'doing' for so long. I needed to develop a lifestyle of resting in God's presence and enjoying His joy.

The revelation of joy rooted itself deeper when I had an accident one evening. I was rushing down the stairs rather fast and suddenly twisted my ankle and fell to the ground. At that point two things happened. My foot started to throb in an excruciating manner and at the same time the joy of Jesus fell on me with great power. I couldn't stop laughing and I couldn't understand the combination with the obvious pain in my foot!

At the Accident and Emergency department at London's Chelsea and Westminster Hospital, I noticed the nurse's quizzical look. 'Are you in much pain?' she asked.

'Yes,' I said with a smile.

She was very confused. 'You are smiling, dear, and you have pain?'

'Yes, both together!'

As I went home I reflected on what I would have done as a *swami* during such pain. I would have tolerated it in my own strength, putting on a façade to show that I was at peace and accepted my body's reaction. This was a new scenario where God Himself had intervened. It reassured me that He would be there in any situation of my life.

Chapter 28
Bethel

At one of the church meetings the speaker, Giles, mentioned Bethel Church in Redding, California. This church has an incredible teaching and healing ministry, and people from all over the world attend Bethel for their own breakthrough in emotional and physical health.

That night Masood turned to me and said, 'Rahil, we need to go to Bethel!'

Masood played a pivotal role in my walk, ensuring that I attended ministries where I would acquire healing at all levels, a heart for worship and a deeper revelation of the Father's heart. I turned to him and smiled. 'Mate, with my earnings, I can just about make it from Mayfair to Brixton!'

He laughed and said not to worry about that. 'I'll pay for the whole trip and even your accommodation and food bill while you are out there!'

I was blown away. 'What?'

He continued, 'Be blessed, mate!'

I stumbled over his offer for two weeks but then I acquired an excitement to go. I was grateful to Masood, but I found it very difficult to receive love and favours from friends. The mindset from my *swami* years was that love had to be earned and I would have to perform for it. I stopped many friends in those early months from loving me. The other reason was that I didn't love myself enough, and so if anybody got too close to me I would find a reason to move them away. Deep inside I believed that I didn't deserve to be loved. All the luxuries and comforts I had enjoyed from friends as a *swami* were from a place of worthiness, as I believed I had earned them through hard work, sacrifice and pouring myself out for the people. Being loved as I am, as a son of God, was still way off my radar.

I was excited for my trip to California and ready to travel once again. It felt a little strange as I had not been on a plane for over a year. There was a time before that when I would be travelling once a week.

I had the most comical moment as I came to the Virgin Atlantic Airways counter. 'Mr Patel, you've been upgraded to business class.'

That was so funny! My first flight after leaving as a *swami* and I was in business class again. I started laughing and said to God that He had a real sense of humour! He replied, 'I can do anything for you!' That was a very special moment as I was still processing through my heart the guilt and shame of the lavish travel I used to have, and so felt that I should never travel like that again. God didn't think so, though.

This was my best flight ever. I felt His presence all the way. I sat there struck by the wonder and mystery of this beautiful new God who was meeting me in so many different ways. My journey had brought me to a smooth rhythm of not trying to figure God out or place Him in a box. The beautiful contrast here was the deep inner freedom and joy as I allowed myself to submit to the mystery. It was different from what Guruji had said. The 'not asking questions' in the climate I had been in had been riddled with control, whereas the surrendering to the mysterious ways of God in Christ was full of wonder, adventure and a deep inner freedom.

I spent two weeks in this beautiful place filled with hungry, loving people and surrounded by a range of snow-capped mountains. I spent afternoons and evenings soaking up God's love and enjoying the views of the landscape around me.

The community at Bethel was incredibly loving, generous and welcoming. It was as if I had walked into a family that had known me for years. There were no agendas or motives: a community just wanting to love unconditionally, without any judgement.

I had Sozo prayer (the same meaning as the Salvo prayer, 'to be saved, healed and delivered'). After two hours of prayer and forgiveness, I found further freedom in my heart.

After a few days, Masood arrived and we attended the graduation ceremony for the 2,000 students who study at the Bethel School of Supernatural Ministry. That evening, Bill Johnson, the senior pastor, gave a word to the students: 'When in doubt, worship.' That word became my new mantra: Worship. It was here that a deeper passion to worship the Lord was birthed.

I sat there on the balcony with friends and suddenly the 2,000 students began to sing without any instruments about their desire for God's praises to ever be on their lips. It was a heavenly sound and God's presence fell powerfully. We were all in awe of the way we were being filled with the Lord's glory. I had tears of joy flooding down my cheeks, as I had never done before.

Never had I felt such a deep sense of God's tangible presence as I did that night. It was here that I received a further revelation that our senses are designed to recognise His presence. For years I had been taught to shut them down – touch, taste, seeing, hearing, smell. I had spent a hard disciplined life trying to numb my feelings through meditations, fasting and chants. I had been taught that the body was to be discarded, ignored and made very tired, so that I wouldn't feel the lustful effects of the flesh. But now I began to comprehend that He designed my body exactly how He wanted it, and that it is beautiful in His eyes, and He wants me to feel Him. My senses were designed to recognise Him.

During my stay, I pondered over the *swamis* I knew, especially Raj, and friends such as Priyam, Pratap and Anil. I thought of all the efforts and strains they were enduring to have God in their lives when He is so readily available through Christ in the most physical, tangible and beautiful way. Again I thought, if only Raj would get this, it would transform his life radically and he would see for himself a new creation in front of the mirror – without any effort, without any work.

My two weeks were over and I didn't want to go back. It was heaven on earth. But when the Lord says to go, you go!

I arrived back in London and my friends saw the change in my face. The beauty was that I hadn't done anything but spend time and 'be' with Him.

After my time at Bethel, I had a sense that God would take me into deeper understandings of this Father–son relationship. My years as a *swami* had been filled with orphan-hearted behaviour. I had been an orphan for so long, and one of the traits that showed it was the fear of lack in any area of my life. My behaviour was also linked with the fear of not being known or acknowledged. The gathering of things in my suitcase and cupboards came from the fear of maybe not being able to buy those things the next day. Orphans always hoard things. They collect objects and grab attention from people. They gain their identity from all other things but God.

I was overjoyed that Jesus gave us the promise in the book of John that He would leave us as orphans no longer (John 14:18).

Chapter 29
Identity and sonship

The year continued to flow with the same rhythm. Work was stable and a blessing, whilst the transformation and healing progressed further. The fullness of joy in His presence was a daily occurrence, and my heart was becoming more and more thankful.

'Though you have not seen him, you love him,' said Jesus' follower Peter. 'and even though you do not see him now, you believe in him and are filled with an inexpressible and glorious joy' (1 Peter 1:8). That was what I was experiencing.

My rent tenancy was ending now in Brixton and I was in search of a new place. I sat on my bed one morning and said to God that I'd like to be close to my workplace in Mayfair, and close by my church in South Kensington. But I continued that I had limited finances and to stay close to these two neighbourhoods would be extortionate. I left my childlike request to Him and wondered where He would send me.

David knew I was searching and so we were both praying. One day he received an email from an established musician who was looking for somebody to stay in his apartment in South Kensington. I went to meet the couple. Both husband and wife sat with me for a while and said, 'We like you. Would you stay with us?'

'Yes!' I said and walked away with another astounding miracle. I was now paying in South Kensington the same rent as I was paying in Brixton!

Although, surprisingly for me, by now my love for Brixton had grown. I was fine with the area and had even thought that I could stay there permanently – and just a few weeks later, God called me to South Kensington. He had completed His work in my heart and had shown me what I needed to see and experience. The journey with Christ was a journey of refining the heart.

This inner journey of my heart being refined developed further through my experiences in the house group started by my friend Jessica Evans. Among this incredible group of brothers and sisters, very early on, I began to notice certain behavioural patterns in me that were not healthy.

I had encounter upon encounter with Jesus, as I have described, but my affirmation and worth came from community and friends, more than from Him. There is a fine line here: we need one another to walk this journey, but above all Christ is the One whom we need at all times, all day, in every situation. I wasn't in that place yet. I needed to be a son.

As I hadn't yet accepted Him as my everything, I noticed myself gaining my identity from friends and ministry involvement. So I was afraid of losing them. Within the intimate climate of the house group I was constantly ready for rejection and abandonment, and so I found myself playing 'safe'. Although I had taken good steps into vulnerability, my heart still had very smart walls around it to keep me secure.

I had improved vastly since my first year, but when it came to deeper levels of intimacy I noticed myself being offended by certain things and yet pretending not to be. This aspect of pretending, hiding, and keeping walls up was at a very subtle level and only the Lord could deal with it. I found it easier to reject a friendship before I was rejected. I sat with the Lord and asked Him what was happening. He told me that I still didn't love myself enough and because of that, when others tried to love me and come very close to my heart I would conjure up ways (at times without knowing) to jeopardise the relationship.

This lack of healthy intimacy with friends was also a reflection of my intimacy with God. I was constantly asking for prayer from people. This was totally fine, and we all need covering and backing with honest vulnerability so that friends can pray for us. But I noticed that I was asking for help from friends more than I was from God. This led me to realise that I still didn't trust Him with every aspect of my heart and life. There was still a deep distrust and fear in going to Him with all of my heart's questions.

Miriam suggested that it would be good for me to do the Bethel Overseas School in London. This was the toughest and yet most rewarding season of my walk as now began the deeper work of identity in my heart and life.

The Bethel Overseas School in its first year deals mostly with identity. The whole course is designed to help identify behaviour that is not Christlike and then allow the Lord to work on it. Identity in Christ alone then leads to healthy relationships and friendships. The bottom line throughout the course is to bring a deep revelation that all our needs at all levels must come from Jesus alone.

Until now I was enjoying His joy with encounter upon encounter, and that would continue. But now the Lord said, 'Rahil, I want you to be a son.' I was, so I thought. But all the phrases I had in my head about being a son needed to move deep into my heart.

One of the things God revealed to me during my time at school was how a name is precious and valuable, both to me and to Him.

I had had problems with my name from childhood. As a child my name was Mitesh, a name I never liked. It mattered to me that I never liked it, but I never told anyone. At school the teachers couldn't pronounce it, and neither could close friends. So people called me Mits, which was fine.

When I entered into *swami* training I became 'Trainee No 5'. A few months later my number was changed to 31. At times when a list was read out for chores the mentor would just read, 'Numbers 1–67 will go to the farm today for cotton picking.' No name would be read. You are just a number when things need to be made easy and quick.

In my first year my clothes, prayer kit and whatever else I was using on a daily basis had my number written on it, never my name, Mitesh. The reason was that when I would finally be ordained that number would be given to another trainee along with the prayer kit and other things I had been using, and I would be given a different final number. In this way my identity would be passed on. So I was a number for a while – first number 5, then 31, then after ordination, 665.

Finally, when I was ordained, another name was given to me that I didn't like. I then told Raj and close friends that it was best that they call me Mits. My passport still had the name Mitesh Patel.

So I was Mits, Mitesh, 5, 31, 665, *swami*, priest, *sadhu* and monk, or Mr Patel for British Airways!

A chaotic confusion and mix! Nowhere was I a child of God. A professional speaker, developer, fundraiser or diplomat were other names given to me, but nothing of a name that brought me significance in God.

This confusion with my name did not allow me to connect with myself or bring a constant rhythm to my existence. When the boy from the Fossil clothes shop shared his name that day, a peace fell on me that assured me that I wanted that name. Rahil would be my name, and I loved it.

Alongside the deep confusion of name changes, my dress code changed from normal civilian clothes to white robes in my first year of training, and then to orange robes when I was ordained with a shaven head. That was for all of us. We all ate in similar bowls, we had similar names, similar clothes, chronological numbers and we all had the same title and surname after our ordained name – *Das* ('servant').

So when I became a *swami*, like all the others, I was stripped of my identity as a unique individual and had to become part of a sophisticated system. You don't realise at the time in the euphoria and excitement, but that's what actually happens. You are asked to erase your past. You own nothing and your identity is tethered to the organisation, its beliefs and culture. You think and conform accordingly. I was taught back then that I had to forget everything about myself – forget my unique likings and dislikes, forget my individual opinions, forget everything about Mitesh. In fact, I was reminded by Guruji time and again that 'Mitesh is now dead'. This belief would please God, and as a result help me find Him.

For this reason my journey with Jesus initially was uncomfortable as I was learning from sermons that He knew me by my name. My name mattered to the Lord. My individuality and uniqueness were important to Him. He knew me personally, as I was.

For 20 years as a *swami* I was focused on forgetting my childhood and background. All the emotional links had to go. On top of the mess that made for me, the day I left as a *swami* my existence from the organisation was erased again! You can see how much confusion my head and heart were in. My identity as a child of God needed to be affirmed, and a deep revelation in my heart of the nature of my heavenly Father needed to be established.

Although many know this truth, the revelation has to sit in the heart and not just the head. That journey from head to heart was very uncomfortable for me, as the teachings revealed time and again my orphaned behaviour as opposed to the attitude of a son. This revealing can beautifully upset you. It did me.

Chapter 30
Healing and deliverance

My forty-second birthday was celebrated in February with a small group of friends, and there I mentioned that I didn't want to continue school. They knew that the discomfort of working on deeper wounds and lies about my identity was the reason. Jessica, myself and two other dear friends, Chris Hall and Charlie Arbuthnot, sat together to discuss my continuing. Their final verdict was to push on. They wanted me to gain more and more inner freedom, however much I was being troubled by the talks and teachings. I agreed, and so the journey of my heart being refined continued to pick up speed.

Experiencing the Father's Embrace by Jack Frost was a book study which brought to the surface the deep-rooted 'performance' issues I had in connection with religion, rules, formulas and theories about God. As these were unearthed and dealt with I felt as though I had gone through heart surgery. Allowing the Lord to bring me to a place of rest and just 'be' took me a while. However, the fruit was immeasurable.

I began to learn that 'rest' is when we are in communion with God at a deep level of intimacy and relationship. I was struck by these words of an older writer about:

living union and communion with the exalted and ever-present Redeemer ... He communes with His people and his people commune with him in constant reciprocal love ... The life of true faith ... must have the passion and warmth of love and communion, because communion with God is the crown and apex of true religion.[2]

This is actually the longing in every person's heart, whether we realise it or not – to have communion with God. That is how God made us. We are designed to be dependent on Him and to have communion with Him. We long for this, but how do we find it? The good news is that we find it when Jesus comes to us in His love. He offers us forgiveness, opens free access to God and gives us His Spirit to fill and change our hearts.

Jesus' follower Paul prayed for his friends that 'the eyes of your heart may be enlightened' (Ephesians 1:18). Timothy Keller explains this:

The heart is the control centre of the entire self. It is the repository of one's core commitments, deepest loves and most foundational hopes that control our thinking, feeling and behaviour. To have the 'eyes of the heart enlightened' with a particular truth means to have it penetrate and grip us so deeply that it changes the whole person.[3]

---

[2] John Murray, quoted by Timothy Keller, *Prayer: Experiencing Awe and Intimacy with God* London: Hodder & Stoughton, 2014, p.16
[3] Timothy Keller, *Prayer: Experiencing Awe and Intimacy with God*, Hodder & Stoughton, 2014, p.20

So Paul's prayer is for 'a more vivid sense of the reality of God's presence and of shared life with him'.[4] This is what I was longing for and beginning to grasp.

I also read *The Supernatural Ways of Royalty* by Kris Vallotton. It spoke to me powerfully and showed me how I had a poverty spirit. I threw the book at my bedroom wall in rage. I was brought up in abundance and had abundance as a *swami*, so how could I have a poverty spirit? I was very upset.

I then realised from the revelatory teaching and my behaviour patterns how much that was true. The book poked at me in a good way! So I picked it up again after a few days. By the time I had journeyed to the end of it, I was a different person. I had begun to move from behaving like a pauper to behaving like a prince. The heart and mind of a prince is very different. I began to live out of abundance instead of a fear of lack.

Gradually, I began to realise the truth of what Paul describes in the Bible, of being a 'new creation' in Christ (see 2 Corinthians 5:17). This whole year was a deep inner work of Christ in me to change me further. All that was not of God was being shovelled out in truck loads! It was tiring but hugely rewarding. I began to sit with more comfort in a place of sonship.

Further progress in this area arose when Randy Clark and Leif Hetland came to London and delivered a conference on healing and sonship. It was a fascinating teaching explaining the behaviour of an orphaned heart accompanied by an orphan spirit. I knew by now that matters in my heart had radically changed. My response to people and intimate situations was very different from just a few months before. My becoming a son meant everything to God:

---

[4] Keller, *Prayer*, p.20.

> You did not receive a spirit that makes you a slave
> again to fear, but you received the Spirit of sonship.
> And by him we cry, "*Abba*," Father.' The Spirit
> himself testifies with our spirit that we are God's
> children.
> *Romans 8:15–16 (NIV 1984)*

My affirmation now came from who I was in Him. Not what
I did. Not which ministry I did or which people I knew. Simple.
Just in Christ. Who am I? I worship Christ. That's where He
wanted me and that's where I ended up. What do I do? I worship
and love the Lord.

I became rested and rooted more and more, feeling His love.
Being still and not letting my mind race to the next thing was
something I had tried all my life through various techniques but
without success. Jesus entered into my life and now the deep
stillness, peace and rootedness were wonderful.

During times of quiet I would visualise the cross. I could see
Jesus upon it, nailed and crucified. I didn't think mentally upon
the act, but allowed my heart to absorb that one very significant
step that He took for me. Yes, it was for my sins – I realised
again how I needed forgiveness. But it also showed how much I
am worth to Him. Nothing could compare with that. My sins are
washed away and my value and worth are reinstated in God's
eyes.

Sometimes I would even visualise holding Him, just like the
statue of *La Pietà* where Mary holds His slain body. I feel the
holes in His hands and feet. The hole in His side pierced by a
spear. This isn't an intellectual thought or idea in my head, but a
connection I allow my heart to bridge. During this I would feel
a deeper sense of His presence fill me. It's a very deep and yet
powerful sense of protection and connection I get with my

Father. I would ask for deeper revelation of the blood of Jesus that was poured out for me.

In this season of inner change, my body now needed to be weaned off a muscle relaxant drug called Lyrica. There was a time when I thought this medication would be with me for life. But God gave me the wisdom to ask the doctors for help, and with a decent plan over six months I came off this complicated medication once and for all without any side effects. Another miracle! After 20 years of travelling the world with a medical box filled with tablets, I had no medicine on me any more. The list of endless illnesses was cancelled by Jesus in just two years.

One last piece of healing I needed was from abdominal pain, and I was introduced to a physiotherapist at Chelsea Westminster Hospital. Another miracle took place here. As the sweet and gentle lady asked me questions, I felt in my spirit to ask her if she was a Christian.

'Yes, I am!' she said with a smile.

I said, 'I am, too!'

We had a long chat and shared our journeys. Clare knew HTB and very quickly became a dear friend. She had received the job as head of the clinic only two weeks before I was asked to visit, and my name 'accidentally' came on to her list. I was meant to be with another doctor. We both knew it was God's design. The healing in the abdomen that hadn't taken place in the Mayo Clinic for ten months took place in six months with only once-a-week sessions of Clare's therapy. It was something I just could not believe and neither could she. There were all sorts of ideas about my abdominal area having surgery, but God used Clare to heal me.

After the summer came to an end, I was feeling better and better. My spirit was more alive than ever and my heart was in a beautiful place.

One Sunday, however, I was leaving church and two dear friends, Robyn and Jonathan Tan, met me and we began to chat. They had played a key role in my journey along with my other friends.

Robyn asked me, 'How was worship at David's Tent?' David's Tent is a 72-hour worship gathering in the countryside of England every summer. Worship leaders from all over the world attend and lead the worship while several thousand people engage with the heart of the Father.

'It was great, Robyn. Yet I still feel a sort of eerie feeling of fear deep in my stomach.'

Jonathan looked at me and said, 'Rahil, there are deeper levels of fear that are unearthed and realised as we encounter more of the Lord's love. Just stay with it and keep worshipping.'

I immediately realised what he was saying. This kind of fear is a spirit from the devil. I saw very quickly how the devil was throwing thoughts of fear across the battlefield of my mind so that I would continue to live life and see the world from that stance. My understanding of fear's dimensions were growing further as I was encountering more of the love of Jesus.

Jonathan continued, 'Don't focus so much on what the enemy [the devil] is doing to bring you into that place of fear. Stay focused on Jesus and keep receiving His love. Rahil, the deeper levels of access the enemy is using to bring you to that place of fear will be uprooted, don't worry.'

This simplified for me the issues of spiritual warfare, and things deeper in my being began to change further. It was strange that as a *swami* I hadn't acknowledged the supernatural realm. I had seen demon-possessed people but always thought they had mental issues. Now I understood more clearly. I slowly began to see the access points the devil was using to bring me fear, and instead of overanalysing I worshipped more fervently.

Another huge space in my inner being was made for Christ to reside, in further and greater capacity. I was blown away with the reality and dynamics of the two tangible realms operating around my life, and became more and more thankful that Jesus saved me.

Thus 2014 was a year of physical, emotional and spiritual healing and cleansing. Week after week on a daily basis I spent more and more time with the Lord and so I received increasing encounters of His love and fire. That fire from heaven was changing all the decay, hurt and unbelief.

I knew that this journey of taking off layer after layer would be God's work and not mine. I unlearned doing the work and began to rely on Him.

Chapter 31
Reflections

In October 2014 I felt ready to go on my first-ever mission trip. Dominic Muir, who is a dear brother in Christ, visits India every year with a group called Now Believe. I am honoured to be a member of this community, a group that is passionate to preach a pure and authentic gospel filled with the fire of God.

I was surprised and sweetly shocked that my heart was ready to go to India on this trip in February 2015. Before that, I hated India: the culture, the attitudes, the land and everything associated with South Asians. I was uncomfortable with my ethnicity and I never quite easily called myself an 'Indian'.

As a *swami* I kept my distance as much as I could from that land. If I were to attend a meeting, I would make sure my flights were back-to-back with the conference dates so that I was in India for the least amount of time possible. My intense health problems, as well as the struggles I had faced there, led my heart to harden towards India. There were horrible memories and I vowed once I had left Guruji in December 2011 that I would never go back. I was done with India.

Like many other facets of my heart, Jesus healed that hardened part far sooner than I thought. I was shocked with my own excitement. If people who were around me during my years as a *swami* saw just this one part of my transformation, I'm sure their jaws would have dropped. 'Rahil? Like India? Never!' Everyone knew my dislike for the land, as I made it obvious. But Jesus can do anything.

This trip was life-changing. Four hundred people turned to Christ during our two-week stay and we saw radical healing and deep spiritual changes. I was comfortable and rested in the environment. I wasn't annoyed by the slowness, chaotic streets and crazy shops. In fact, I was wonderstruck with the vibrant colours and lush countryside. I fell in love with the village people and ate the tasty food they made. I was surprised at my change and the natural way I was enjoying and laughing at every aspect. I look forward to my next visit.

I'm very thankful to the Lord that He reconnected me to my land of inheritance. I realised in a new way that when I was baptised it wasn't a rejection of my family and community. I didn't need to lose my culture. In fact, now I was connecting with my heritage in a much deeper way, beyond my experience at any time in my life before. London is my home, but I know that I belong to India as well.

A beautiful addition within these two weeks was my birthday celebration. Very early in the morning Dominic and the whole team, one by one, looked me in the eye and told me why they loved me. We enjoyed a lovely cake. Then, on top of all that, my dad phoned and told me he was so proud of the work that I and my friends were doing. And he added, 'I'm really happy that you have connected with India as well.'

By God's grace I have come a long way in a very short while. I haven't had the chance to sit and process the whole transformation, as I feel my mind doesn't have the capacity. My mindset, attitudes and perception to life and people have changed drastically. They have changed just by sitting with Him and worshipping, and not by my own effort: no earning, no working.

I was stripped of everything once I left Guruji – all the material things and fancy titles that I had clung to for years. In the midst of having nothing, God gave me a powerful encounter that overlapped everything I had and permanently changed my perception of my destiny, which is to worship Him here on earth and to live for eternity. In one single moment, Jesus changed my whole worldview.

I had tried so hard to reach God by my own efforts. I thought my achievements would somehow please Him and win His favour. Now I realised that I could never reach Him that way. But Jesus had taken my place. My standing before God now rested on Jesus. In Him God forgave me, received me as a son and showed me all His favour. All I had to do was receive.

In that moment of encounter I had nothing to my name. At that very naked time of my life, His encounter clothed me with the nourishment I had needed for years. This stark contrast of having being stripped bare and on the other hand having a touch of His love gave me the clarity and focus I needed to pursue Him as the only source of joy in my life.

This was important, as the idols in my life were not only the other gods that I had worshipped but idols of titles, status, famous friends and material things. I clasped them to justify my existence whereas He wanted Himself alone to be my justification. I'm so thankful that the Lord stripped me of everything and gave me Himself alone.

With Him at the centre of my life and my only source of affirmation and justification, I feel more and more rooted. I am a lover of community and 'family', but my sense of worth comes from the Lord

I have certain healthy dreams and aspirations, such as my own home, but not at the cost of eternity or His presence. I'm hoping to be patient in my wait for the Lord to provide. He has been faithful thus far and He has never failed me.

Jesus has made me so comfortable, rested and at ease. I'm fine with not being 'someone' with a title or position, but a son and a child of God. That's a tectonic shift in my mindset. It doesn't mean that I will not pursue a career of any sort that He may suggest. It means it will not happen at the cost of my being a son or my heart being positioned in Jesus Christ at all times.

My time at the London Bethel School brought such a deep healing that I am now in a place where I want to love people without condition. I don't try to give away love to my friends with a hint about having it back. I try to rely only on His love daily and from His river to love all those around me. I am dependent on Him alone.

I know how I am when I haven't spent time with Him, in His love. I'm not good. This realisation has brought me to a beautiful place of complete dependence. I am reliant on Him throughout the day for my soul to be continually nourished. He meets all my needs and I try with grace to live my life with that heart, always rested in Him.

As a *swami* I would skip my morning prayers and various *artis* and *pujas* of worship that others greatly valued. If not, I would speed it up to get it over and done with. Now, I look forward to my time with Jesus in the morning, and times of corporate worship. I enjoy it, I thrive on it, I live for it. It's not a religious rule or discipline that I must do, but a moment that I'm excited about, as I meet with His deep river of love. While at work I look forward to finding a space to sit with the Lord and enjoy Him. He is so attractive. Whatever the challenges of the day, His faithful, tangible love always settles and roots me well.

I have a handful of fears and anxieties about certain aspects of my life, but compared to the level they were before I can honestly say they are minuscule. They don't send me into a spiral panic of restlessness. When they arise, I know where to go. I go to Him. I have an honest conversation with Him, and His faithful love roots me back into heavenly perception.

Along with my reinstated love for India, I have grown back to loving the colour orange. After I left being a *swami* I didn't wear anything of that colour. Even though I liked certain orange clothes when I went shopping, I didn't buy any and I wouldn't dare to wear them. The association with my past was too much. The Lord healed me of that and I enjoy wearing my orange shirts and ties!

I'm enjoying the mystery of journeying with Him without any sceptical mindset. He is Truth and so I'm not worried any more. I enjoy asking the Lord what He is doing for me today and He reveals to me where He wants me to be – in the present. It's not always easy, as I do rush into the future, but when I come back to where He is I find rest.

I remember being so restless and unable to be still, always thinking of the next thing to do, the next place to go or the next person to meet. Now He is gradually bringing me to the beauty of being present in every moment.

I see the pattern and rhythm in His ways. But I'm also aware that if the pattern changes the Lord knows what He is doing. This is a peaceful trust that I have in Him. If at all I have a fear of 'What will happen next?' I sit with Jesus and He brings me the peace and trust I need.

There are still areas where I would love to trust Him more, and I know He is helping me. He is a Father. My life has been taken out of a box and is full of adventure and exciting anticipation.

I am thankful for the smallest of things in my life, as well as the bigger blessings. I am also thankful that Jesus healed me from shame, guilt, resentment, bitterness, anger and so many hurts from my past. He is the Healer. I am thankful that He is changing me and has given me a forgiving heart.

When I think back over my years as a *swami*, I do thank God for many things that help me today. The organisation sent me to some wonderful places, from Istanbul to Lake Victoria and the source of the Nile. I'm grateful for all those cities, towns and places I got to explore, and the exposure to nature, from the mountains of Colorado to the stunning Swiss Alps. I value the friends of those years and remember them with affection. I remember the hundreds of families I met and ministered to. The insight gained from sitting with each one gave me a huge advantage in comprehending various dimensions of family life. Working with very clever board members and understanding the intricacies of running a massive organisation were a huge help. I can see the benefits when I sit with friends today who run various charities or businesses. My training years, although not fun, did give me a grounding in some important matters, such as maintaining confidentiality and avoiding gossip. I learned disciplines that still help me today.

Again I am thankful for the healing in my body. After my return from India, my metabolism increased to the level it had been when I was 15 years old! I now cycle every day to work and run twice a week. I no longer have high cholesterol or body pain.

Most of all, I am thankful that He waited for me for 20 plus years and never gave up. He kept knocking on the door. I'm grateful He chose me and called me. I look back and see how Jesus had His eyes on me all the time, waiting, knocking patiently.

I look back at my journey with delight, and it has been adventurous and fruitful. He will use what He feels He needs to use from my past for His glory and kingdom. I have no idea which aspects, but I know He does. So I'll sit patiently as He unfolds that to me.

I'm thankful for a radically loving community to assure me that we are together on this great journey we call life. More than anything, that Jesus Christ is with me and my friends, all the way. I am beautifully overwhelmed by the person of Jesus. Through Him, I am now a son of my heavenly Father. Though for many years I ran away from Him, He kept searching for me and now I am found. He was searching for me all the time. I am thankful that He found me. My Father. My *Abba*.